To Faris.
There is
to explore
story of o...
Roselm

THE
ORDINARY
TURNED
PRECIOUS

a quest for belonging

Roselle M. Gonsalves

THE PATIGAN GROUP

www.rmgonsalves.com

Edited by Lindy Pfeil Hughes (www.lindypfeil.com)
Author photo by Luminarie Creative (www.luminarie.ca)
Book cover design by 100 Covers (www.100covers.com)
Typesetting & interior book design by Dustin H. Smith

ISBN: 978-1-7380911-0-2 (paperback)
ISBN: 978-1-7380911-1-9 (ebook)

This story is the truth as I remember it. All the interactions and conversations contained in these pages occurred, though names and identifying details of most living individuals have been anonymized or changed. To respect the privacy of those who may not wish to have their lives so publicly exposed, I have on occasion combined two or more people into one, or altered the chronological sequence of events. Speaking my truth while also honouring my commitment to not perpetrate harm has been an intentional act of compassion, both towards myself and others.

www.patigangroup.com

THE
ORDINARY
TURNED
PRECIOUS

a quest for belonging

Roselle M. Gonsalves

GRATITUDE TO PLACE

My roots run deep in the earth of the Konkan coast, and my lineage stems from multitudinous directions. I was born and raised at the edge of the ocean in Bombay, where my patrilineage connects me to the Koli Tribe, a fishing people who live by, with, and on the ocean. My blood and bones will always be baked in sunshine and enveloped by salty sea breeze.

My adolescence and early adulthood were spent on the shores of the majestic Lake Ontario, on land that is the ancestral, current, and future home of the Mississaugas of the Credit First Nation, the Haudenosaunee Confederacy, and the Huron-Wendat and Wyandot Nations. My mind and heart have been shaped by this land, upon which I absorbed the value of seasons; that it is only in shedding its fiery orange leaves and taking time for a winter's rest that the majestic maple return strong and proud the following year.

My adult life has been a blessing given to me at the feet of the indescribable Rocky Mountains, in a place known as Moh'kins'tsis, which exists at the confluence of the Bow and Elbow Rivers. This fertile place is the homeland of the many peoples of Treaty 7, including the Blackfoot Confederacy (comprised of the Siksika, the Piikani, and the Kainai First Nations), the Tsuut'ina First Nation, and the Îyârhe Nakoda (including Chiniki, Bearspaw, and Goodstoney First Nations), as well as the Métis Nation of Alberta Region 3. I continued to build my life in a place called ᒥᐢᑲᐧᒌᐧᐋᐧᐢᑲᐦᐃᑲᐣ, amiskwacîwâskahikan, a traditional meeting ground, gathering place, and traveling route of the Nêhiyawak (Cree), Anishinaabe (Saulteaux), Niitsitapi (Blackfoot), Métis, Dene, and Nakota Sioux.

It is in these places that I have found the courage to nurture safety, the medicine of good relations, and the ability to reach up to the neverending and piercingly blue sky to ask for healing.

My home now is in Mi'kma'ki, the ancestral and unceded territory of the Mi'kmaq people. Here, I have returned to my deep ocean roots, knowing that ocean people tell long stories of journeys to distant shores, so that we might remember lessons from long ago and for ever.

I am indebted to the generations of Indigenous peoples who have cared for these lands since time immemorial. Thank you for shaping and stewarding the spaces in which I have been afforded roots, reflection, and repair. I will strive to permeate this inheritance bequeathed upon me onward...in all my relations.

for her
for you

NOTE TO READER

When this story began shaping itself into a book, I wanted to tell it for two reasons: i) to bear witness to myself, particularly to the parts of myself that had never felt the sun shining down on them; and ii) to have my stories bear witness to those who, like me, have been taught to be ashamed of their own stories.

The experience of writing this book has allowed me to see myself and the beauty of my life in the most profound ways. I hope that somewhere in these pages, you too feel seen.

The book has been written in a voice that is most authentic to who I am in this world: including multiple languages. In order to create clarity for the story, I have offered accessible translations for most non-English words. However, where a translation is either unnecessary or non-existent, I have left the words to stand on their own. More often than not, context will create clarity. However, if it does not, I invite you to lean into the discomfort of not being centered in the book as an empathetic bridge to the experiences of people who live between multiple languages everyday.

Finally, this book deals with some difficult topics, including but not limited to child abuse, emotional and psychological abuse, alcoholism, and dysfunctional family dynamics. There are also brief mentions of self-harm and suicide. As you read, please care for yourself in whatever way is best for your own wellbeing.

TABLE OF CONTENTS

PROLOGUE

Prologue

"Aashaa,
gushaa,
aaaaaa."

Papa and I giggled these nonsense syllables together
as he doused me in a delicious stream of perfectly warm
water from a bucket. Enthralled, I sat on the bathroom
floor as my 80-something-year old maternal grandfather
sat on the commode, bathing me and getting sprinkled
with the resulting splash himself. This is my oldest and
most precious memory.

Papa lived with us. I had never known it any other
way. He and Achie had the smaller of the two bedrooms
in our flat in Bandra, a seaside suburb in the city of Bombay. Achie is Papa's youngest daughter, and my godmother. Between them, I was showered in love, certain of my

place in the world as a first-born daughter, a golden child, the one onto whom they could pour all their love, like the warm water from the bucket. Together, they made certain I knew with unwavering clarity who I was to them, and how much they adored me.

My second oldest memory is of being perched on Papa's ankles as he lifted his legs in the air with me going along for the ride. I giggled hard. His face was lit with utter joy as I bobbed up and down in the air on my human see-saw.

I was Papa's eighth grandchild, and arguably (this was my argument, of course), his favourite.

My mother was Papa's eighth child. In total, he had ten children through two marriages. Later in life, I would learn that his own children perceived him as beloved, albeit distant and stern. To me, he had hung the moon.

Papa was the eighth, and final, child of his own parents. Born after seven sisters, he was the exalted golden son yearned for by his parents, and upon whom all their wealth and belongings were bequeathed.

By family lore, Papa wanted none of his birthright, leaving his Goan village of Ucassaim for the bright lights of Bombay in 1918, at the ripe age of 18, chasing his dreams of being a musician.

All of this would come to my knowledge much later. For now, in these memories, he remains just my Papa. Excellent at baths and human see-saws, soft of word and gentle of manner. He was a safe spot in my world, which would soon lose so much of its softness and safety.

These precious first memories of my Papa and myself are encapsulated in that perfect space between the before-time, of which I have no memory, and the after, of which it may be time to tell.

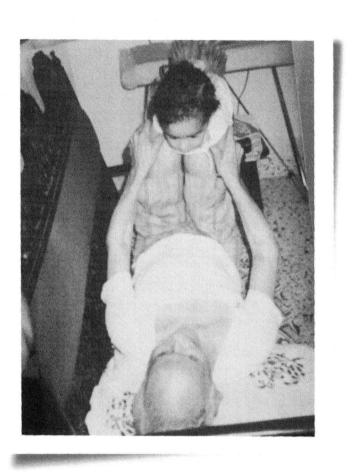

I don't feel that it is necessary to know exactly what I am.

The main interest in my life and work is to become someone else that you are not in the beginning.

If you knew when you began a book what you would say at the end, do you think that you would have the courage to write it?

What is true for writing and for a love relationship is true also for life. The game is worthwhile insofar as we don't know what will be the end.

—Michel Foucault
"Truth, Power, Self" Interview, 1982

Roots

2008

Where Are You *Really* From?

"I don't want to go to India, mum. I hate it there."

The first semester of graduate school is coming to a close, and over the last few years I have been highly successful in moulding my life into a product of creative nonfiction: reality heavily augmented by the illusions of perfection found only in indie films.

"You need a break from school, Roselle. Come with me. It'll be a good rest for you."

"I'll rest when I'm dead," I quip back.

This conversation with my mother in her kitchen is frustrating. It risks bursting the bubble that ensconces my finely crafted life. I roll my eyes as far back as they go in response to my mother's coaxing.

My perfectly-curated life sees me often strolling through the Annex, the Toronto neighbourhood in which

I live, Billy Joel's "Only the Good Die Young" scoring the background to the tedium of trekking to the laundromat. Fresh bagels win my last few dollars rather than toilet paper, because it feels so romantic to be broke but eating fancy bread! It doesn't matter that my poky little studio apartment smells perpetually like gerbils, thanks to the fur shop atop which it sits. Nor does it matter that I work three part-time jobs on top of a full-time academic course load. I tell myself and anyone who'll listen that I am happy beyond measure, albeit always over-caffeinated and under-rested, which seems to be in fashion at 23.

"Why do I have to come with you? I just don't like going back there."

"You haven't been back in so long. It's nice for you to go, no? Everyone asks about you."

It's true. I haven't been back to the place of my birth in nearly a decade, and if I have things my way, I'll be happy to never return. India is not for me, and it has been made abundantly clear that neither am I for India.

It is dissonance realized to live in the space between not belonging to the place where I was born and continually being asked where I'm from in the place that I now call home.

✳

Having moved to Canada from India at age thirteen, the question of where I'm from has been a regular part of my life since then. In all that time, I've never truly explored the many ways in which I could respond to it. The truth is that there are many times and places from whence I've come forth, in which I am rooted.

Sometimes, this query is an invitation to find relation. Many years from now, I will find the most profound instances of this when engaging in my doctoral research. "Where are you from?" Mrs. Pinto, one of my research subjects, will enquire. "In Goa, I mean."

"My Papa, my mother's father, was from Ucassaim. We're from Bardez side. But he left for Bombay long time ago. My mum and all her family were brought up in Bombay."

"Oh, yes! Our family was from Aldona. Side by side to Ucassaim…we must be cousins!"

The nugget of personal geography that I offer to Mrs. Pinto allows her to deduce that my ancestors were part of the earliest high-caste Goans converted to Catholicism in the 1500s, under the missionizing Portuguese colonizers.

The details about my ancestry serve to validate my religio-cultural identity to Mrs. Pinto. Though time and space have separated me from those roots, to her, I belong.

In this instance, "Where are you from?" builds a sense of belonging in an ocean of being "other." This, however, is not always the case. Often, "Where are you from?" takes on a barbed edge; an accusation of eternal un-belonging.

✳

The orange leaves had already begun their annual descent to the ground. My friend Amit and I sipped our over-priced lattes at a shop in the Annex: warm bougie comfort from the rainy Toronto autumn and the doldrums of grad school. We did that a lot back then: working in hipster coffee shops, waxing poetic about the world and our lives in ways that were only possible in our early 20s, when we were grad-student-poor and vocabulary-rich.

I had met Amit on our first day of graduate school at the University of Toronto; he was starting his doctorate, and I was yet a lowly master's student.

"Hey, I'm Amit! I spent the last year of my MA in Mumbai, and I'm here to start my doctorate in Hindu Studies," he'd said by way of introduction to the group. Immediately my ears perked up.

"Hey!" I approached him after the group intros. "You said you'd spent some time in Bombay recently?"

"Yes! Have you been?"

"I was born there. Whereabouts were you?"

"Oh, I lived with a host family in South Mumbai. I even picked up a bit of Marathi. Do you speak?"

"No way! That's my grandmother's native language."

"*Mala sabji payje*," he blurted at me.

I giggled because he'd just told me that he wanted vegetables. It seemed to be the only Marathi phrase he'd retained from his time in the city of my birth.

"*Majhe nav* Roselle *ahe*," I introduced myself to him in a tongue I hadn't used for years.

We giggled, and a fast friendship that still remains, was born.

At the Annex coffee shop, we distracted each other with banal chit chat.

"So, what does your family speak at home then?" Amit asked.

"We've always only spoken English. My mom and dad also only speak English, except with certain family members. My dad spoke Marathi to his mom, and my mom speaks Konkani to her relatives. They don't share a language other than English."

"Wow! You really are Macauley's dream child, aren't you?"

"Who?"

I had no idea what he meant, but I sensed there was a pointedness to his jest. It spurred me to dig into this

Macauley character, whose dream had allegedly come to fruition in me.

Thomas Babington Macauley was a British politician. As part of the Indian Education Act of 1835, he wrote a memorandum on Indian Education that would become instrumental in the implementation of English education in India under British rule. In it, Macaulay writes:

> *We must at present do our best to form*
> *a class who may be interpreters between*
> *us and the millions whom we govern;*
> *a class of persons, Indian in blood and*
> *colour, but English in taste, in opinions,*
> *in morals, and in intellect.*[1]

My friend Amit had been born in the southern United States and raised in New England within his devout Hindu, Gujarati community. He fit every Western notion of what it means to be Indian. I, on the other hand, though born and raised in India, spoke English as my first language. My diet had never been religiously shaped, and my family's Catholicism was five hundred years deep.

I had *never* been the right kind of Indian.

My command of the English language, a colonial tongue, is owed to Wren & Martin, and far supersedes my knowledge of the three Indian languages of my ancestors: Hindi, Marathi, and Konkani. I can recite Shakespeare and Keats, but not the *kavyas* of Sanskrit scholars and poets. I even dream and sleep-talk in English. I have a colonized mind, and though I have worked hard at undoing the practice of grammar-policing, it is still my first instinct to be annoyed at incorrect grammar and syntax. I know now that these ways of thinking are rooted in the

1   *Speeches by Lord Macaulay with His Minute on Indian Education.* 2013. England: Taylor & Francis. http://www.southasiaarchive.com/content/sarf.145158/.

British cultural superiority that Macauley professed; that they create racist, classist, and ableist impacts. I know it will be a lifelong tussle to weed out the spaces within my own mind where these vestiges of supremacy reside.

I know that Amit didn't intend to hurt me at that Toronto cafe, and years later when I would recant this moment to him as a pivotal point in understanding my own identity, he balked. However, by reducing my identity to the product of a Macaulayan effort, I had been left to interpret that not only was there a correct way to be Indian, but that even in the diaspora, my expression of Indian-ness wasn't it. My very existence had been reduced to a calculated product of colonial whims, disallowing any agency on my part—I was the victim of colonialism, and had I known better, I would have chosen to be a true Indian. This idea was echoed years later by another Indo-Canadian acquaintance who would deride me for belonging to a community that had allowed ourselves to be colonized.

"I guess I'm just really proud that my family didn't let ourselves get colonized, like some others," she would hiss in my direction.

Her righteous moral superiority stung like lash marks left by the whip of lateral violence, reminding me, as I'd been reminded my whole life, of my role as "other."

✱

Having grown up in Bandra, an idyllic little suburb of Bombay on the shores of the Arabian Sea, where generations of my ancestors had fished for a living, I was a *bindaas*, care-free, child. School and church were a short walk from home, and all our neighbours shared our religio-cultural stripes. Roaming the streets of Bandra, I made friends with strangers, most of whom seemed to be related to me in some distant way, all of whom knew who I was and where I belonged. It was easy to forget that we were religious and cultural minorities, vestigial remnants of Portuguese colonization: English-speaking, booze-drinking, meat-eating, liberal Catholics who were incongruent with the wider ecosystem around us; predominantly Hindu, conservative, teetotaling, vegetarian, fully Indian.

In 3rd standard, or grade 3, a child psychologist had assessed me as intellectually gifted but academically bored. This combination erupted in chattiness in class, an inability to sit still in my seat, daydreaming, not applying my potential. So, in grade 4, my mother removed me from the all-girls Catholic school with all my neighbourhood friends. Instead, I had to take a 40-minute ride on a school bus to an academically rigorous private school in a posh part of town, with privileged kids from all backgrounds, most of whom had been there since kindergarten. I may have been academically ready for the new school, but I was ill-prepared for the social integration that had also come with the move.

It was a Scottish missionary school with a British education curriculum. In addition to my healthy love of the bagpipes, it also incepted me with values that further served to separate me from my Indian-ness. For instance, in our school agenda, a reminder from Lord Nelson on how to govern time:

"I owe all my success in life to having been always a quarter of an hour before my time."[2]

I knew not who this Lord Nelson was, but his words, printed in the agenda and imprinted onto me, meant that

2   *1820 February 26, The Ladies' Literary Cabinet, Volume 1, Number 16, Edited by Samuel Woodworth, Anecdotes, Quote Page 126, Woodward & Heustis, New York.*

I would forever be early to everything. This resistance to tardiness continues to make me subject to much teasing from my *desi* peers for not following Indian Standard Time, which runs anywhere from a half to two hours late. My sense and governance of time have been forever coloured through a colonial lens, and I wept in adulthood to read *Latitudes of Longing*, in which Shubanghi Swarup questions who governs time, and why the meridian passes through England in the first place?

At my new school, the first part of our lunch break was for eating. The rest of it was for playing outside. One lunch break, I sat alone in the back of the classroom. My hot lunch was usually a lovingly-curated version of the previous night's dinner menu from home. This particular day, Achie packed for me her decadent Beef Rolado—a Goan version of the German Rouladen, where tender slices of beef are wrapped around veggies and tied together to simmer in a rich gravy. Achie used twine to secure the beef around the veggies.

I was acutely aware of Mrs. Aadekar, my grade 4 class teacher, at her own desk, surrounded by a gaggle of her favourites, all of them watching me. Head down, I concentrated on the meal in front of me; Achie's food never failed to bring me warmth and joy.

The twine that held that day's lunch Rolado together needed to be untied, and I was tempted to pull at it with my hands. My dad called eating food by hand, "*ghatti* behaviour," meaning that it lacked class or civility. Even though Indian food tastes best when hand-eaten, Dad insisted that we use utensils at all meals, and I didn't want to appear uncivilized at my new fancy school. Unable to untie the twine with just my utensils, I reached into my backpack for a pair of scissors to make light work of that which stood between me and Achie's delicious food.

As I snipped the twine, Mrs. Aadekar spoke, "Look…just look at that savage, cutting her chicken with a scissor."

The whole world stopped as peals of laughter erupted from the children around the teacher's desk. Hot tears started bubbling.

"It's not chicken," I sputtered, my throat choking with emotion.

Surely if they understood that it wasn't chicken, but twine, then I wouldn't be a savage?

For the rest of my time at that school, I was remembered as the girl who cut chicken with scissors. After that, I rarely, until well into adulthood, felt comfortable eating in public. In the years that followed, Mrs. Aadekar would be only one in a choir of adults at my new school who would reinforce for me that my family and I didn't belong in India. We were foreigners. That is, of Western origin. I was Mother India's illegitimate child: a shameful remnant of a torrid affair, no longer wanted and best forgotten.

✸

As I stand in my mother's kitchen now, attempting to get out of going to India with her, wave after wave of the shame of unbelonging washes over me. How do I convince my mother that I've reconstructed my fully-Canadian life here with no wiggle room in it for some other place? That I don't want to go to India because India doesn't want me?

This tragic poetry of being India's unwanted child found its echo in the resentment-filled amniotic sac of my very incubation. I came to be in that grief-filled year in my mother's life when she should have been able to experience her own heart breaking in mourning her own mother's death, but instead had to use her life's energy to incubate me. For this ultimate price, repayment with compound interest continues to be extracted.

As my mother continues trying to convince me to go to India with her, the undertone of her argument becomes decidedly guilt-inducing.

"You owe me," she says in not so many words. It is the underpinning of our entire relationship, this high price that she has had to pay so that I may exist.

At best, the emergence of my existence had been a heartbreaking inconvenience. My mother will tell you that she hadn't yet known she was pregnant with me while her own mother lay at death's door. Omai had refused to lay her head on my mother's lap that night, pointing to my mother's stomach:

"*Phutele*," she had said.

(It will break.)

How Omai had known that there was a delicate lifeform to protect, my mother will never know. Omai died later that night, leaving her middle daughter eternally aggrieved that the fetus within had cost her that final tender moment of maternal connection. I continue to be reminded often of this high first price that my mother paid so that I could exist.

In the Space Between

"Mo-o-o-o-mmmmm. I have so many papers to finish right now, mum."

"Yes, yes, papers I know. But you need a break also no? And you get time off after the semester? It'll be nice for you to come with me."

My mother is still insistent that I accompany her to India over the upcoming Christmas break.

"I can't think about the break right now, mom. I don't understand what we're going to get done in six days there anyway?"

My mother doesn't care for my refusal, so she tries a different approach.

"It'll be better if you come with me. I need your help with the house matters. The lawyers have finally drawn up all the papers and I think we can get the deal done with the buyer. We just need to get all the signatures. Please, you haven't come to India for so many years. Every time…"

"Mom, I hate going there. None of my friends are there anymore! My life is here now."

My attempt to interrupt my mother's verbal speed train is futile, and she continues as if my words are soundless.

"…every time, I go by myself, and I have to do all this heavy work by myself. There's no one to support me and I have to make sure that all this work is done. This house has been a headache on my head for 20 years now and I'm not even the one benefiting from it. You're the one benefiting from it - I'm doing all this running around for *you*."

Her emphasis on the last word is purposeful. With it, I am reminded that I owe my mother for my very life.

The house that my mother is referring to is the ancestral home of her father, my Papa, which was bequeathed, as part of his estate, to a number of his children and grandchildren upon his passing in the late 1980s. While I am one of the named beneficiaries, along with a few of my cousins, uncles and aunties, my mother has been named the executor of Papa's will while inheriting nothing of his actual property and assets. In hindsight, that division seems rather absurd, but that's neither here nor there.

For nearly three decades, Papa's children haven't been able to agree on what to do with the house and property in Goa, which has remained uninhabited for the better part of a century now. Some want to sell, some want to contest the will. Having been four years old when Papa died, I have formed no opinion on the matter. I'd have gladly traded all my share of the property for more time with him, the most special person in my young life.

I can feel the beats of my heart racing up into a hum,

filling my ears. My ability to express that I don't want to go is stymied by my inability to process all of my emotions in this moment: despising India, missing Papa, wanting desperately for my mother to get off my back so I can go back to pretending I am a short, brown-skinned Jack Kerouac, writing poetry and smoking cigarettes in maudlin coffee shops, waxing philosophical about the world's problems.

Ol' Jack doesn't have to worry about the old country. He is counterculture *within* his culture. I can't be one of his mad ones, burn burn burning like a fabulous Roman candle if I keep being dragged out of this well-crafted version of myself to some previous iteration of who I'd been in a time and place I am working very hard to forget. This version of me does not want to have tethers to that other culture…the one from before when this me came to be.

The humming in my ears is even louder now. I cannot think past the emotional response to flee and hide from this place, which demands that I be physically here while being simultaneously tied to somewhere else.

✸

My mother's voice fades out over the loud humming in my ears, and my attention turns to my shallow breaths. In my head, I start chanting a Sanskrit mantra that I've recently learned in my yoga classes.

Om Namah Shivaya Gurave
Saccidananda Murtaye
Nisprapancaya Shantaya
Niralambaya Tejase
Om.

The sounds are familiar and foreign all at once, Sanskrit being the proto-language of all the Indian languages I know and am desperately trying to forget.

The first time I heard the chant, the teacher had sung the words to open the class. Her lullaby had soothed me and my body sank deeper into the ground, buoyed only by my sweat-stained mat. I had been on this mat daily for 26 days, something I had felt pulled to almost as if by a force outside my own body. Toronto's springtime had been damp and cold; the kind of damp cold that clawed its way past a jacket and burrowed into bones.

The upcoming autumn was spiriting me away to the unknown frontier of a master's program. In the space between a cold spring and an unknowable autumn, I had felt the urgent need to ground myself in something, anything. A local yoga studio had been offering a 30-day pass for a price that suited my impoverished student budget. So, there I was, humming along to a Sanskrit mantra, ready for a sweaty 60 minutes of physical, spiritual, and emotional grounding.

"Breathe in," lilted the teacher, as I forgot how to process breath, and breathed out instead.

"Fill your lungs with as much love and oxygen as you possibly can. Then ho-o-o-old. Just hold. As your lungs hold, listen to your body...not your mind. What is coming up in your body?"

My body did not care for this intrusion and attention.

The teacher continued, "Can you ease its tension, its fear? Listen to your heart beating. Ba bump ba bump ba bump. Today we focus on the heart in our practice. Today is all about *anahata*."

As I moved my cranky body in that heated yoga studio, the teacher accompanied the *asanas*, poses, with teachings about *anahata*, the heart space, which is unhurt, unstruck, unbroken.

A heartbeat is just as much about the thump-thump-

thump, which is audible and accessible, as it is about the spaces between each thump...the silent spaces between the notes that give them meaning, rhythm, cadence. That day, the teacher had invited us to imagine filling these silent spaces with our breath energy, for it is in cultivating the heart space that we allow the loud beating audibly accessible parts of the heartbeat to have more meaning, more strength and vitality.

✱

The anxiety of existing in the space between acquiescing to my mother's request, and my deep desire to never return to the place of my birth has been a constant in my life. Once, on a family trip to Goa, while chatting with a fruit vendor in Konkani, the language of all my maternal ancestors, the vendor responded, surprised, *"Foreignsaan ailein, pun amchi bhaas khub bori uloitha!"*
(You've come from abroad but you speak our language very well!)

I was both thrilled and deflated at the *fruitwali's* comment, which would place me firmly in the category of "foreigner;" an outsider who'd found lingual in-roads, but an outsider nonetheless. The interaction would be a mirror to the numerous occasions in Canada when I've been asked if English is my primary language, or why I speak it so fluently if I am a first-generation immigrant. I am eternally in the space between an identifiable other in both spaces, and quasi-belonging to both/neither.

This lack of fully belonging to either space, Canada or India, was born through my immigration to Canada at the age of 13. I had lived in India long enough for it to have an indelible impact on my heart, mind, tongue, tastes, language, and values. Yet, as a child immigrant, the move itself had not been a choice for me. Over time, I have become too Canadian to ever return fully to the land that bore me, and having been born somewhere else, my Canadian-ness will always hold the turmeric tint of my Indian roots. Culturally, I often feel like a child of divorce: one whose parents have remarried different people, and have had new children with their respective spouses, leaving me quasi-belonging to each family, and still somehow belonging fully to neither!

✳

The humming in my ears drowns out my mother's natter, and I focus on my breathing and the spaces between the breaths. Slowly the rushing in my ears dies down, and my mother comes back into focus. She's still trying to convince me to take this trip with her.

"Come on baby. It'll be so nice for us to go home at Christmas, no? We haven't had that in so long."

Her use of the term "go home" makes me wince, but I am too drenched in the torrential downpour of my emotions to articulate that the trip doesn't feel like an act of going home to me. I remember with piercing clarity, the exact moment at which India, the place in which generations of my ancestors had been born and raised, stopped feeling like home.

✳

It was two days before my First Holy Communion. My pretty white dress and veil had been stitched. I had been itching to wear the pearl white tick-tock shoes that Dad had bought me, but Mama told me they needed to be perfectly white for my big day. I was so excited, I could barely stand it, because Mama had said I could use her shiny silver wedding purse! I even had lace gloves.

Mama had asked a family friend to prepare *fugias* and a suckling roast pig for my big day. We weren't going to have a big party like the other two kids in the building who were also receiving their First Holy Communion. They were set to have parties on the terrace and in the compound. Instead, Mama had invited a few people, mostly family, to our house. I secretly wished I had been able to have a party, but Mama said that Dada would be tired and that a party wasn't the point of this holy sacrament.

Aunty Maureen, my Catechism teacher, who had gotten us all ready for the big day, had asked us to arrive at the church for a final rehearsal with our parents. Dada had just arrived home from the rig and so couldn't come to the rehearsal. I was worried he wouldn't know the right steps, or when to turn, or what side of me to stand on. But, he would be there on the actual day of my Communion and that's all that mattered. Mama had been at work all day and so she wouldn't be at the rehearsal either. Aunty Maureen pretended to be Mama for the sake of the rehearsal and had put me in charge of remembering that Mama needed to be on my right, and Dada on my left. Or vice versa. I forget.

Achie had been at the *bazaar* and picked me up after rehearsal. She was frantic when she arrived at the church.

"Come baby, there were some bombings, you know. The *bazaar* is closing. Let's go home."

Achie and I walked home quickly as shopkeepers all around us shut down the metal roll-down gates on their shops. Achie clutched her packet of groceries tightly in one arm and held onto me much harder than usual with her other hand.

I didn't understand. "Achie, what happened?"

"You know these people, men. They bombed a *masjid* somewhere, you know. They're saying now they're coming here. There's going to be a *bandh*. Come quickly, let's go home."

The entire neighbourhood was aflutter. Dusk was falling, and as we arrived at the gates of our compound, Mama rode up on her scooter, from work.

"The trains were packed," said Mama, handing Achie a packet of fruits that she'd bought on her way home, "Everyone is trying to leave town."

I didn't know whether to feel scared or excited. I suppose I felt a bit of both.

Dada was still asleep when we got home; his *nasha* from the afternoon drink would have just started to wear off. Mama woke him just as air sirens blared through the streets of our usually sleepy suburb.

"Fill all the buckets with water," Mama instructed Achie. "Did you buy enough meat at the bazaar?"

"We have enough food and the gas cylinder is full," Achie assured her.

Within hours, the air sirens were all we could hear as we remained glued to the television. Just that past year, I remembered us doing the same thing and watching the oilfields of Kuwait burn an eerie neon green. Dada had called that the "Gulf War," which had scared me because I knew he worked on oil rigs in the Gulf somewhere, and I hoped his rig wasn't anywhere near those bombs.

Mama said that when she was small something similar had happened, and that they had to black out their windows. We drew thick curtains over all our windows and dimmed the lights to be safe too. Mama and Achie made sure we had batteries in the torches and enough matches for candles if needed. Mama tested the emergency battery-powered lamp in the cupboard that we'd never used before.

My friend Ronnie came to the door of our flat: "Come come. We're all going to the terrace. The *gundas* are setting the Bandra station on fire. We'll be able to see it from up there."

Ronnie lived on the fifth floor, just one storey lower than the terrace level, so he knew where to look. Mama told us not to take the lift, so we ran up the stairs, huffing. We grabbed our friends from the building on the way up. It was exhilarating. I had never seen the whole building so abuzz. Except that one time a few monsoons ago, when all the roads had flooded and we went bonkers when a neighbour arrived at the building in a dinghy that he'd pinched from a *machchiwali*, fishmonger, in Chimbai.

I didn't see when Dada arrived, but all of a sudden he was on the terrace with us too. We all stood watching, agog. The adults were trying to identify what was ablaze. Dada said it was the *musalmaan* wood marts by the Bandra station. The flames were bright and had a green tinge to them, just like the Gulf War fires I had seen on TV the year before. I didn't want to look at it for too long.

"Why are they burning the wood marts, Dada?"

"I don't know, *boochie*. Something must've happened."

It was difficult to go to sleep that night. The adults were wound up, and I wanted to stay up and make sense of what was happening. My perfect little corner of the world would never be the same.

The next morning, the world was eerily silent. One of the thick curtains had blown open in the morning air, and I peeped outside. Everything seemed fine, normal even. Something felt off though. It was a little too silent. Which, in a city like Bombay, was not a rarity so much as an impossibility. Dada went out first thing in the morning and bought the morning *Times* at the newsstand because our daily delivery hadn't arrived. Achie complained that the milkman also hadn't shown up.

Handing me a Complan milk instead, she declared, "There's a *bandh*, no school today! Drink!"

I pored over Dada's shoulder at the newspaper, trying to see what on the front page had him so engrossed.

"These *chutiyas*," he grumbled under his breath, sipping his Nescafe.

"Is this in the real Ayodhya?" I asked. The only Ayodhya I knew was from the stories of the *Ramayana*, my favourite of the two great Indian epics. I had no idea that it was a real place.

"It's all nonsense," Dada muttered, more to himself than anything. I didn't understand what he meant, but I nodded along sagely as if I did. The situation seemed to call for me to be somber.

Dada's childhood friend, Uncle Saleem, came by, and together they left. Dada said he was going to check on what was open. Mama yelled at him from the bedroom, "Check on the bazaar and buy some fruits and milk if they have some. Get *kanda-lasoon*, just in case too!"

A few hours later, Dada returned, smelling of whiskey, which belied the detour that he and Uncle Saleem had taken to the Casbah, a local Bandra watering hole.

"The bazaar is completely shut down," he reported, dropping a bag of onions, garlic, and meat on the dining table. "I got these *kanda-lasoon* and some mutton, but *gundas* are starting to loot the shops that are open, so I couldn't get anything else. Everything is closing. No pork or beef at the meat market either."

"What about the *fugias* and suckling pig? Did you

go there?" asked my mother.

"Their house is in the dark, they don't have any power, and they can't get the suckling for tomorrow. Nothing, there's no beef or pork anywhere. But they had these ready," replied Dada, pointing to the bag of freshly-made *fugias* that he'd also brought back.

"Don't worry, baby," Achie piped in, sensing my distress at the news that the special food for my party was in jeopardy. "I'll make a nice green mutton curry for you, and peas pulao. It'll be nice," she assured me, handing me a still-warm *fugia* from the brown paper bag on the table.

Word in the building was that the other parties were going to be canceled. There was a rumour that the city was going to put a curfew in place.

Over the weeks and months following the night on which I stood on the terrace and watched the Bandra wood stalls burn, we lost family friends in bombings. Uncle Saleem stopped coming over after dark; it was no longer safe to be outside at nighttime, especially if you were identifiably Muslim. The supplies of produce and meats dwindled. Even the *machchiwali* aunties were being harassed as they went about their days, selling fish, which had become the only non-veg food option available.

We shared in whispers with neighbours the cautionary tale of four teenagers, three Muslim and one Hindu, who hung out after their college classes and got attacked by a gang of rioting hoodlums. All four were killed in the attack, the underlying tragedy being that the goons had killed one of their own, a Hindu boy, in their blind rage. It stopped people from mingling in mixed groups, lest they become the next victim of mistaken identity, as if the tragedy of the young Hindu boy was any less or more tragic than the deaths of his three Muslim friends, who had also been murdered. It sowed seeds of division that permeated the cultural firmament forevermore.

Within a few short years of those events, the landscape of India, which had always been a pluralistic space, would become decidedly unwelcoming to religious minority communities. By 1995, just three short years after the destruction of the Babri *Masjid* in Ayodhya, the cacophony of voices telling us to leave India had become overwhelming. I didn't understand any of it and wasn't entirely clear on why some adults had taken to telling me that I wasn't really Indian.

At eight years old, I didn't understand the politics or the ensuing violence. I just knew I was scared, and the only place I knew as home had started feeling like an ill-fitting, misshapen, once-favourite sweater: familiar and foreign all at the same time. Many of my friends were scared too. Everyone was on edge, and nobody wanted to say the wrong thing because we'd all heard stories of friends turning on one another, tossing each other out of windows.

When my family eventually moved to Canada a few years after the riots, in an attempt to wipe my own slate clean, I too would toss a part of myself out of a window.

✴

That my mother is now asking me to return to India with her as a way of going home feels vile. For me, India is something to erase. It symbolizes rejection, and I am not about to return to a place that doesn't want me. On the other hand, my mother's version of India has a much longer arc. To her it always will be home. As she pleads with me, I can hear her longing for the place she remembers, and the ache of loss at having to relinquish it for the promise of a better, safer life here in Canada. I am hyper aware that I am only afforded this Canadian life as a direct result of her loss.

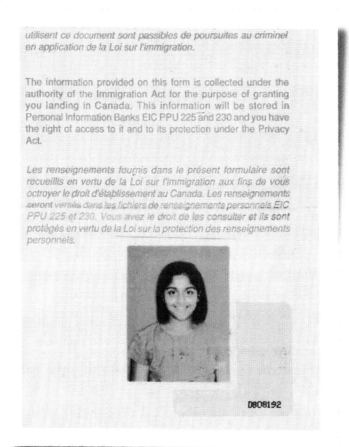

We spent our first nights in Canada in an apartment in Toronto. I was amazed that every bathroom seemed to have a tub—a luxury I had only ever seen in American movies. I entered my first grocery store (an IGA!) and was enthralled by Red Delicious apples, which looked picture book perfect. Everything was so clean and orderly. It was a stark distinction from the place I had called home my whole life, where people were ubiquitous, social order was a theory, and traffic lights offered mere suggestions. I missed the chaos and the din of life that never stopped in Bombay. The order and superficial perfection of my new home space invited my adolescent self to step into being my own perfect self. If I could excise all the messy, noisy, chaotic parts of myself that had made it so difficult for my mother to love me in India, maybe I could re-emerge as a picture book perfect child in this new place. I would be the Red Delicious apple of daughters.

Two weeks after we landed, we got SIN and health cards, and went looking for a new home to purchase. In the interim, my family and I moved to Port Credit, a bucolic waterfront area outside of Toronto, on the shores of Lake Ontario. The water wasn't salty like I had been used to growing up, but I was happy to have it close by nonetheless—it felt familiar. We stayed in a long-term hotel called the Ports Hotel, a relatively well-kept building with bright blue balconies, right on the water, across from Scoops Ice Cream, a neighbourhood highlight.

I started school at St. Mary Star of the Sea, a small Catholic elementary school where I was welcomed with warmth and curiosity. I loved my grade 7/8 split class, my rad new classmates, my first male class teacher, Friday lunch at Helen's Fish & Chips, and my first foray into learning French. I even joined my first protest march to save the pesky geese loitering on the waterfront from a city-proposed cull! I met another girl who had also recently moved here from Bandra, but she sounded less like me and more like the Canadian kids. I made a mental note to work hard to sound normal. I hatched a plan: normal would be a rest stop on the road to perfect.

My mother was on board with my plan to reinvent myself. In those first two weeks of being in Canada, she found me writing in my trusty diary, a practice I had for many years despite knowing that she read my private thoughts regularly and punished me for them viciously.

"Enough with all this now, huh?" She snorted at my writing, waving a derisive hand at my diary. "Now's your chance to turn over a new leaf, and leave all this nonsense behind you."

I really wanted to commit to being a new, perfect, lovable girl, but I was also gutted at the prospect of having to relinquish all the treasures of my old life. My precious diary contained notes passed in secret between friends, a Valentine's Day card from a crush that captured all the bittersweetness of being a 12-year-old in love. My diary also taunted me with all accounting of my past sins and transgressions. It seemed to hold all the reasons why I needed to start anew, and one afternoon, I felt compelled to rip out all the pages of the book that had held my secrets for so long. I stuffed the pages into an envelope, sealing it so my secrets wouldn't spill. I didn't want to be that version of myself anymore; I wanted to be fully Canadian, not stuck in the space between here and there, bad and good, before and after. Standing at the fifth-storey window of the Ports Hotel, I tossed that loaded bulging envelope into the giant garbage bin in the hotel parking lot. My aim was true. Now I was free to reinvent myself. All accounting of who I had been was gone.

Everybody is Somebody's Villain

"Mom! I can't! I want to take time between my semesters to prepare for the new one. I have a full course load, and I need a break. Please don't make me go!"

My argument is becoming repetitive, pleading. Surely if my mother knew my reasons, she'd understand why I cannot go and would stop haranguing me?

Try as I might though, my mother is adamant that I accompany her to India. My mother is always quick to remind me of the debt I owe her for the opportunity to even consider the reinvention of myself; reminding me often that my self wouldn't even exist without her input!

"You wouldn't even be in this country going to your big fancy university if it weren't for me. I sacrificed everything for you. You can do this small thing for me please!"

The sacrificial lamb is owed an eternal debt, and my

mother is fond of extolling the costs that my existence has taken on her life and choices.

"I was a queen at home, now I have to slave here because of you."

"You wanted this house, so don't blame me now that you have to clean it."

"I came to this country for you."

✳

I left my parent's home for the first time at the age of 18. intentionally choosing a university where I could live on campus. It was the first time since moving to Canada that I felt free. In those first few months of living away, my mother sent me email upon email lamenting my abandonment of her; cruel epistles denouncing me as no longer part of the family, letting me know that I had chosen the outside world over her love. Informing me that I would never truly find belonging outside the walls of the home she'd created for me.

By the third month, my mother informed me that she was leaving for India for an eight-week trip, and that it would be my responsibility to drive multiple hours daily between university and home to ensure that my 12-year-old brother went to school and guitar lessons and swim meets. I found myself juggling a full first-year course load, living away from home, wanting to hang out with my friends, and also commuting hours each day on Ontario Highway 401 from Guelph to Mississauga, so that I could quasi-parent my brother. Over the two months of doing this, I didn't miss a single school drop-off, swim meet, or guitar lesson. Nor a single class of my own.

By the time my mother returned from India, I was exhausted beyond repair.

"See? It's not good for you to live so far from home. You're burned out," my mother expressed astutely upon her return. "Come home no? Transfer to UofT. I'll buy you a car if you do. It'll be good for you."

I acquiesced.

The next fall, I transferred to the University of Toronto, hopeful that living closer to my mother would quell her fears of abandonment.

My hope was short-lived as my mother announced at the end of that summer that it was unfair that I had benefited (in stark contrast to her sacrifice) from her decision to move us to Canada. She quit her job to enroll at a local college.

Rather than doing her own school work however, my mother put her assignments and papers on my desk. In her mind, not only had she birthed me, but she'd also sacrificed her cushy life in India for my sake. The costs she'd incurred for my benefit were to be paid for by me doing her assignments.

I was at a new school, trying to enjoy a 19-year-old's social life, working two part-time jobs, and managing a full course load. My mother was indifferent to these considerations.

"Please. You're so good at schoolwork. You can write these in no time; you're already doing this for your classes. Just copy and paste for me."

"I can't mum, that's plagiarizing."

How could I make her see?

"See? You know such fancy words. You wouldn't even know them if it weren't for me. I've helped you your whole life. You can't help me out just this once? You gave me such headaches when you were small. Just do this small thing to help me, no?"

My mother has reminded me often that I am a burdensome bad seed, a difficult child to love, a problem to solve.

She has worked hard to solve me.

✳

My mother was a cruel parent to me. Whereas my father was mostly absent, and his rare presence often whiskey-soaked, my mother was actively antagonized by my mere existence. To be sure, my mother had very much wanted a child. But I wasn't the child she had hoped for.

Some of my earliest recollections are of me being bad. I don't recall what actions of mine yielded this label, though I'm sure I was as frustrating as any other three or four-year-old. Almost daily, I was sent to kneel in the corner of the living room, a healthy layer of coarse salt between my young knees and the tile floor. I would stare at the candles burning on the side table, trying not to shake too hard from the salt crystals burning into my skin, silencing my sobs to not make things worse.

"Mama please let me get up. I have to make *susu*. Please Mama."

"You don't have to make *susu*. This is all *natak* so you don't have to kneel," my mother would jeer.

I would hold my bladder as long as I could, but inevitably, I would release it on myself. The thick yellow urine ran down my thighs and melted the salt crystals that had started to draw blood from my knees. Blood and urine combined in a pool around me.

Sometimes, before this could happen, Achie would come pick me up from the corner.

"Enough now, huh?" she would say to my mother as she took me to a warm bath.

"It's ok baby. It's ok," she'd soothe me as I wept, not knowing why God had made me such a bad, unlovable, girl. "You're a good girl, baby. You're a good girl."

I never knew what would trigger my mother into punishing me. I was in awe of her cool outfits, her *tick-tock* heels, taking the train each day to town and back, and the barrettes she wore in her thick curly mane. I wanted to be a good girl so she'd love me back. Each day when I returned home after school, I'd work hard to get all my homework done, trying to make sure that everything was in place so I wouldn't incur Mama's after-work wrath. The only thing worse than the kneeling on salt punishment were the canings.

Achie and I would make daily plans for when I would be taken to Mama's bedroom and shown the business end of a whipping cane for my misdemeanours. Achie would coach me:

"You be good, ok baby? Just say sorry so she doesn't beat you more. I won't let you be in there too long. I'll come knock on the door and make some excuse. Be good, ok baby?"

It was a relief when the whip cracking on my young skin was interrupted by Achie's knock on the closed bedroom door. Mama would put the weapon away, look at me disappointedly, then shower before dinner and the daily Rosary, where we'd all convene as a happy family.

Religion was a big part of my childhood. Religion offered not only a faith tradition, but also the underpinnings for my sense of culture, and the value that comes from being a part of a tightly-knit, insular community. This community swelled with pride a few times a year, particularly around feasts that celebrated our unique religio-cultural traditions.

A perennial favourite was Bandra Feast, which began each year on September 8. This was a great community celebration, commemorating and exalting a statue of the Virgin Mary that had been found at sea by local *Koli* Christian fisherfolk, a few centuries ago. Mount Mary's Basilica was built in Bandra to house and venerate the Virgin Mother. It was known far and wide as a special pilgrimage space, and each year people from all over India would descend onto our little suburb for two weeks of veneration, prayer, and celebration.

Carnival style games and rides and booths selling all manner of wares were set up all week long. My favourites were the balloon shooting booths and the stalls selling sweets. I loved the rides, especially the ferris wheel. We didn't call it the ferris wheel back then, but I no longer remember what we called it because linguistic losses are a given component of the cultural loss that accompanies an immigrant's story.

We'd go to the Feast Day mass with throngs of other people. I'd help pick out beautiful garlands of marigolds and lilies for Mother Mary. Each year, I would kneel before the venerated mother, squeeze my eyes tightly shut, and pray fervently to her to please make me a good girl. I don't think my pleas ever got delivered because each year I'd leave the Mass only to head over to the stall that sold canes and whips. In hindsight, I imagine that the stall's wares were meant for cattle. As a child, I thought that all parents took their children there to re-up on the cane that would be used to punish them in the year ahead. My mother made me pick out my own cane each year, making it difficult to complain about a weapon of my own choosing during the subsequent daily canings.

These canes were made from dehydrated sugar cane stalks. Similar in look and density to bamboo, the knots became that much harder when dried, leaving longlasting welts and wounds on tender young skin. If you've ever drunk *ganna* juice, you know the sweet sweet nectar that sugarcane yields when pressed. The pain it yielded when lashed into my flesh was just as potent.

One year, while picking out my cane, I spotted helium balloons at an adjacent stall.

"Mama, Mama, can I have a balloon, please?!"

"Yah, ok," my mother acquiesced, handing a few bills to the vendor selling her my cane for the year. "You can buy as many balloons as you want. Let's see how many you will need to send this cane up to heaven."

This was a tantalizing scheme: if I chose the right number of balloons, we could tie them to the cane that she'd just bought, and send the cane up into the sky so that it wouldn't be around to hit me. I knew that if I asked for too many balloons, I'd be in trouble, so I asked for ten, which felt like an audacious number. I felt mischievously gleeful at the prospect of that fucking cane flying off.

Later that evening, we tied the ten balloons to the end of the cane. I held my breath as it appeared to ascend into the September air. The balloons proved no match for the heavy cane however. I exhaled with a thud as it landed heavily on the ground, and later, on my skin.

✳

My badness permeated all the spaces I was in. The nuns at my all-girl Catholic primary school were as tired as Mama was of my misbehaving. When our class teacher resigned (I had nothing to do with the resignation, I swear!), we had a rotating crop of substitute nuns until our new teacher arrived. In those weeks, I ran away from the classroom often, much preferring the schoolyard jungle gym to the boring classroom, where I was told that I talked too much, anyway. I saw the ends of a few rulers on my knuckles in that interstitial time until Teacher Francesca arrived. Teacher Francesca was tall, with thick black hair and a fringe, something I desperately wanted and was never allowed to have. Teacher Francesca took an immediate liking to me, and I thought she was a princess, with her long nails painted bright red, and her heels.

At one particular Bandra Fair Mass, I prayed loudly to Mother Mary, asking for a baby brother. Soon after Teacher Francesca arrived, my brother was born. Teacher Francesca coached me on how to be a good girl at home so that my Mama could rest and be with the new baby.

Teacher's 26th birthday was approaching, and as a treat, she picked six of us from our class to join her for a special celebratory lunch. Teacher Francesca had her own mum prepare a delicious lunch of beef cutlets and rice pilaf for all of us. I ate lunch with Teacher Francesca and my pals in the classroom that afternoon, feeling bathed in love and delight. This teacher didn't think I was bad, even though sometimes I was too chatty in class.

The daily canings slowed down after my brother's arrival, though they didn't disappear entirely. When I moved to the posh private school in grade 4, my mother did her best to hide the evidence of the beatings, making sure to only cane me above the knees, and on other areas that would be covered by my uniform. I'd sit in class, and every so often lift up the hem of my gray uniform tunic to look at the evidence of the lashes. I would run my fingers across the welts, so I could prove to myself that they existed, that it happened, and that the public-facing gas-light-fueled image of a well-loved child was the actual lie. I would push into the welts to elicit pain, which acted as a grounding rod for my reality.

✳

In grade 6, my badness erupted in an acute way. It began in my weekly elocution lessons at Betty Vincent's house, where I saw a cat-shaped eraser on Miss Vincent's dresser. I swiped it. I got such a thrill from this potent secret! Soon, I was swiping curios from everyone around me: fancy pencils, colourful thread, a stainless steel ruler, a calligraphy nib for my favourite fountain pen. When the machinations of my petty thievery came to light, the cane was replaced with the buckle end of a thick leather belt. Those welts drew blood, and lasted much longer than the others.

My grade 6 teacher, Mrs. John took me under her wing after my brush with kleptomania. She helped me return my stolen loot, and apologize to each person I had wronged.

"You did a bad thing, my girl. But you are not a bad person. Remember that, ok?" She held compassion tenderly beside the need to hold me accountable for my actions.

A couple years after that, when I left that school because my family and I were immigrating to Canada, Mrs. John signed my goodbye book, telling me how proud she was of who I was becoming. She ended with, "I love you."

For decades after, this was the part of my life of which I was most ashamed. It had proven beyond the shadow of any doubt that I was, in fact, bad. Only bad people steal, and my crimes were evidence of my badness. I wouldn't believe Mrs. John for a long time to come.

✳

Long before Mrs. John and my short-lived life of petty crime though, long before Teacher Francesca and my brother arrived on the scene, back when it was still just Mama and Dada and I, I had asked my dad to please buy me a Walkman. I loved listening to music and I loved my mother's sleek black device. I longed for one of my own.

On his next trip home, my dad presented me with a bright yellow Walkman, with a matching headset. I was over the moon, though my elation was short lived as my mother snatched it from my hands.

"I'll take this one, and you can have my old one," my mother said, nodding over to the black piece that she no longer seemed to want.

"Why? Dada bought this one for me," I pushed back. This made no sense.

"You always get the best, and I have the old one now. That's not fair."

A few days after the Walkman fight, from which I walked away triumphantly holding the new yellow one, I rushed home from school excited to listen to my new gadget. I went to grab it from my cupboard, where I'd left it. There it sat, broken into four pieces.

In hindsight, it wasn't fair. I hadn't worked hard to get a Walkman. I had simply asked for one and received it. In the context of my mother's life, that wasn't fair. She'd had to hustle and work hard from the get go; I was handed life. Similarly, I hadn't chosen to move to Canada, and yet I benefited immensely from being here. I wouldn't have those benefits without the choices that my parents made. My privilege meant that I could build my life off the sacrifice of those before me to achieve that which they may have only dreamed of.

✳

As I stand now in my mother's kitchen, being reminded of all that she has sacrificed so that I might have my cushy, downtown life, a Jungian idea that I've learned recently floats into my brain: that the greatest tragedy of every child is the unlived life of their parents. My mother tells me often that my life is the one that she deserved to have. That I owe her. While I have always believed this to be true, I cannot find a way to square this belief with my lack of desire to go back to India with her over the upcoming break, so I shift tactics.

"I don't understand why we need to sell it. Why can't we all just put some money into it and fix it up? We can use it as a family cottage or something for whenever we visit. Then we can all share it: all of Papa's children and grandchildren."

What began as a way to squirrel out of a trip I desperately do not wish to take, is now tumbling out of my mouth as a genuine plea. I realize that I'm not bullshitting.

My desire to try and find a way to hold onto the house that has been in my family for generations is palpable, even though until this exact moment I hadn't known that I cared about it.

The Periscope of Privilege

"All they care about is money!"

Exasperated, I pour myself another glass of wine, and top off Lydia's too. We are curled up on the futon that takes up nearly a third of my gerbil-scented studio apartment. We are going dancing with our friends, and plan to let the Grey Goose and bad decisions drive the rest of the night. I am filling Lydia in on my mother's insistence that I go to India, and my frustration at my relatives being unwilling to save Papa's house, the reason for the trip.

Lydia and I have been friends since we were 13 years old, and she is my very best friend in the entire world. My number one gal, my ride or die.

We met in the late 90s, in our Grade 9 French class. We got along like oil and water. She annoyed the hell out of me. She was perfect where I was messy. She was conscientious where I was careless. She was stoic where I was mischievous. Both 13-year-old nerds, we were each other's toughest academic competition. I loved the thrill of the challenge! Over time, competition has softened into a bone-deep friendship, and we grew up and into one another.

Over the years, Lydia's parents have become my surrogate parents. Her sisters are my siblings. My rudimentary Polish is thanks to her *ojciec* teaching me his beloved mother tongue, most of which revolved around swearing! My love of mushroom pierogies began in their family kitchen. Her family nicknamed me *Różyczka*, and it always makes my heart happy to walk into their home.

Our years of being entwined in each others' worlds meant that we rarely stand on ceremony or tiptoe around the truth. I am being purposefully dramatic and whiny about Papa's house, and Lydia isn't about to let me off the hook:

"If they need money, then what use is the house just sitting there empty and crumbling going to do for them? It's frustrating, I know, but it's easy to not care about money if you've grown up having it."

I hate when she is right. I am uncomfortable with the truth in her words, and perhaps also with my own privilege-laced myopia.

✳

Growing up, I knew that I was a high-born child, heir to the prestige and majesty that accompanied being *Brahmin*, a word whispered as if it were a secret, albeit the world's worst kept one. As Catholics, caste was a non-issue in our lives. Until it wasn't. That is, it suddenly became spoken again when talks of marriage or family status came about.

"Achie, what does that mean, that we're *Brahmin*? Is everyone *Brahmin*?" I once asked out of curiosity.

Achie was unphased by the mighty questions I often asked her, and I could always count on her to take them seriously.

"No baby. *Brahmin* is the highest caste. Higher than all the others. But, we're not Hindu ok?"

I nodded sagely as if I understood. I did not.

The true weight of my caste privilege would not dawn on me until decades later, during my doctoral research, when a research participant, a woman in her 80s, asked me, "Where are you from?" I gave her an overview of my ancestors.

"Ah, you all are Brahmins." She paused, pulling anxiously at her hanky, her words more plea than query:

"Baby, I am not a Brahmin. We are lower. Do you still want to talk to me?"

"Of course, aunty! That doesn't matter to me. Tell me more about your people. I'd love to hear."

Aunty went on to tell me in great detail about the customs of her people, and how they might differ from mine. Her trepidation dissipated as we talked, but I was thoroughly shaken by the deference with which she spoke to me, even though she was my elder. My caste privilege has made me entirely unaware of the weight of it on those who do not have it.

✱

I was raised Catholic, and ostensibly, all vestige of our pre-Catholic cultural identities, which emerged with the arrival of the Portuguese to India, were meant to be erased.

On May 20, 1498, under the auspices of King Emmanuel I, Portuguese explorer Vasco da Gama and his crew, came to shore in south India. When the Portuguese ships, adorned with the crucifix, arrived in India, lore has it that da Gama pronounced proudly to the Indian locals that he had come to India to seek souls and spices.[1] The implication of this declaration being that da Gama's primary goal in coming to India was a missionizing one. My maternal Goan ancestors, from the northern part of the state of Goa, were part of the first wave of this missionizing conversion.

These high-caste Brahmin families were given land, title, status, class, and prestige in return for loyalty to the European newcomers. My ancestors had to forsake their names, castes, religious affiliations, foodways, languages, attire, and all other ties to their pre-colonial identities. The colonial endeavour was an intelligent one: if the most privileged castes were offered even more privilege and dominion, they would be motivated to side with the colonizer over their lesser brethren, since the latter were already viewed as lesser than, and the former was handing out unearned prestige!

Lower caste Goans were not as lucky as my ancestors. Many of them, along with many other peoples from the South Asian subcontinent, were removed from their home place and taken to far-off lands that were also a part of colonial holdings. To perpetuate the myth of racial hierarchy, at the top of which sat white European bodies, and at the bottom of which were Black people of the African continent, brown people occupied the space between: at once recipients and also instruments of colonial violence and myth maintenance. Indians were taken to places like Guyana, Trinidad, Zimbabwe, Uganda, South Africa, Fiji, and Mauritius as indentured servants. In these places, they

1   Fernando and Gispert-Sauch, Christianity in India: Two Thousand Years of Faith, 73.

were simultaneously oppressed by their colonial overlords, and also acted as instruments of oppression towards the Black people indigenous to those places. This anti-Blackness, and corresponding ideas of white supremacy, remain a swift undercurrent that permeates Indian ideas of race superiority, even today.

The descendants of those indentured Indian communities are now generations removed from their home place, cultural outsiders in all the places they call home. My life in Canada has afforded me the opportunity to connect with a number of these distant cousins, all of us now in the diaspora.

In a conversation with my tattoo artist Kee, whose family is from Mauritius, they acknowledge that Indians from India very rarely see them as *truly* Indian.

"Peh! I'm a child of the motherland. You are as Indian as I am. You're my kin," I quip gleefully as Kee smiles and continues pressing the needle into my skin. Brown skin that I proudly share with them, and with the soil from which we both come. The rupture of time, circumstance, and colonial mythology has already done us all too much harm for us to continue to perpetuate that lateral violence upon one another.

Here I am reminded of Audre Lorde's caution that the master's tools will not dismantle the master's house. In her comments on the "Personal is Political" panel at the 1979 *Second Sex Conference* in New York, Lorde implores white women to recognize that their whiteness will not save them from sexism—a luxury that she as a Black woman cannot have. She implores women who hold more privilege to stand alongside their more-oppressed sisters, instead of siding with the powers of oppression, in order to bring about a more just world in which everyone can flourish.

As someone born in the place where my people have been born for hundreds, if not thousands, of years, it is easy for me to grant belonging to those who have not been made to feel like they belong, like my pal Kee. However, my circumstance of birth is no accident; it is a consequence of the privilege that my ancestors had, which I too share. It was this privilege that protected them from being ripped from their homes to a life of servitude in foreign lands. It doesn't mean that life didn't end up being harsh for many of my ascendants. It simply means that the difficulty of their lives was not caused by being removed from our place of birth and belonging.

I have done nothing to earn being born into a *Brahmin* family. And it has very little bearing on my daily life. The privilege I experience is the lack of consideration that I have to give to ever thinking about it.

Where my caste privilege continues to offer me an invitation to unpack its many tendrils, guilt over my socio-economic privilege was what haunted my early years. I hadn't asked for my dad to work far away so I could have nice things. In fact, I'd have rather had less but had him around more. I used to beg for this, only to be told that I was being ungrateful for all that I have. This did nothing more than make me feel further guilt.

As is common practice in India, my family had a live-in maid. Often our maids were very young, some even pre-pubescent. One in particular, Sunita, was barely a couple years older than I was when she came to live with us. I was in the 3rd standard. Later that year I would learn what periods were because Sunita got hers and I wanted to know what all the kerfuffle was about. To commemorate this moment for Sunita, my mother bought her a bottle of body wash. Mama got me one too, so I wouldn't feel left out. A few weeks later, I found that the silky washing liquid in my bottle had been replaced by soapy water, and I had no doubt that Sunita had stolen it. I was enraged at this injustice and marched with righteous indignation to my mum to complain about it.

"You have so much, you should be grateful. It doesn't matter. Let her have it. You can have these things forever. This is just one nice thing she has."

Guilt consumed me for being selfish. How could I feel angry about being aggrieved, when the very existence of my feelings implied that I was ungrateful for the nice things I had?

Guilt is useless though. It implies that I've done something wrong, when that is not the case. Shame is guilt's even less useful cousin. Shame suggests that I *am* something wrong. Even that is not the case. The guilt of having access to resources, where so many around me didn't, weighed heavily on my young heart. It wasn't fair, and there seemed to be nothing to be done to rectify the imbalance.

✴

There is space between being who I am and having what I have, unearned though some of that may be, and acknowledging that these privileges create for me an intended unawareness to the powers that they wield. I have come to recognize that in this in-between space lies my duty to the humans around me: a duty to continually examine my own privileges, and divest myself of any illusion of power and protection that they may bring me, while maintaining between me and another an illusory separation.

My ancestors harnessed their caste privilege to ally themselves with the incoming colonizers, and used that alliance to garner themselves social status, wealth, and power. It gave them centuries of privilege, in exchange for betrayal of their neighbours, and their own identities. When the Europeans left the subcontinent in the 20th century, they didn't care to ascertain which Indians had been their tools, so as to protect them in the subsequent cultural vacuum. The purpose of the tools had been fulfilled. Yet, what remains, in a bizarre version of cultural Stockholm syndrome, is an ongoing rupture from our identities as neither fully Indian, nor anything else really: a colonial invention. The tragic poetry of da Gama's holy mission and McCauley's education system.

On my mother's birth certificate, her father's occupation is listed as "musician." Born to a high caste wealthy Goan Brahmin family, Papa had turned his back on the family bakery business, leaving Goa in 1918, at age of 18, for the bright lights and promise of the fledgling metropolis that was the city of Bombay.

He rented a two-room tenement flat in the South Bombay neighbourhood of *Dhobi Talao*, a place on the shores of the Arabian Sea where *dhobis* made their living by offering laundry services to residents. The tenements were filled with young migrant men from Goa, all seeking to make their lives and livelihoods in the big city.

It was the era of the British Raj in India, and Papa would go on to join the British Auxiliary forces, becoming a well-decorated military bandmaster over the next couple decades until 1947 when the British vacuumed out of the subcontinent, leaving a wake of chaos, rupture, and despair.

In the mid-1940s, Papa became a widower: the death of his first wife left him with the prospect of raising three young daughters alone. Simultaneously, the expulsion of the Brits from India saw his years of military service and pension erased, with very few job prospects available for a military musician in post-British India. Those years saw Papa's family, my family, plunged into abject poverty. It was the kind of permeating poverty that continues to impact many members of my family in all the intersectional ways that bone-deep socio-economic intergenerational marginalization does.

When I think about Papa and the intergenerational tethers that bind us, I am compelled to examine both the traumas and the boons that tie us to each other: what continues to hurt and what continues to benefit me to today. These tethers are the ties that bind me to people who came before me in ways so deep and yet, often, mostly intangible.

✻

Lydia's simple comment pulls into stark focus how my privilege has blinded me to the very real, immediate, monetary needs of my family member who would like to sell Papa's estate quickly. I feel embarrassed that it hadn't occurred to me to grasp the situation from their perspective.

"Just don't forget about me now that you're a rich heiress," Lydia teases me.

Sarcasm has always been our love language, and I know that she is trying to soften the sting of the conversation. I take a big gulp.

"Don't worry. I'll make you my mistress and give you the life of a kept woman in my soon-to-be mansion."

"Perfect. I'll start picking out drapery fabrics."

Our vodka-fueled night of revelry proceeds as planned, and we end up back on my tiny futon afterwards, lulled to sleep by a Polish sausage from one of Toronto's infamous street meat carts.

The following morning, as we sit groaning through our hangovers over brunch at a local diner, we circle back to the topic of Papa's house.

"So, are you gonna go?"

The mid-morning Caesar is soothing my headache, but not enough to mask my annoyance at being prodded about this again.

"Ugh. I don't wanna."

Lydia gives me a look, which brooks no argument. I know she's waiting for an actual answer.

"I've got so many papers that I need to finish. I wanted to relax over the holidays. It's a lot to fit into a week."

My response sounds feeble, even to me, particularly since I've spent the entire weekend cavorting. I crunch into a strip of bacon.

"When do you need to decide by?" She's undeterred by my reasons.

"I guess I should go. I'm just feeling angry, you know? Like nobody else cares that we're giving up this house that's been in our family for so many generations. Nobody wants to save it. And I know it's probably better for them to have the money to use now than have this house be useless and worthless, but I just feel like that's the last thing I have of my grandfather's you know? And if we sell it, then what? I get a bit of money?"

I trail off, deflated.

"How much do you think you'll get?"

"A few thousand dollars? Five or six, maybe?"

We eat in silence. There is a refill on our caesars. Our silences have always been few and far between, so when they appear, I know it means something serious is coming:

"I think you should go. You've never been there."

"I went there when I was very small, right after Papa died. I think my mom told me we couldn't go inside because there were snakes," I interrupt because the small detail matters, if only to me.

"Ok, but you don't remember it much, and it was a long time ago. So why not go and see the house, say good-bye if you guys decide to sell it? Maybe pick up a rock or something from the garden to keep as a token of your grandfather. And if you sell, then maybe take the money and put it in a savings account, so that when you're ready to buy your own house, you can put that money towards it."

Her idea seems so simple. So perfect.

I guess I'm going back to India.

'

Perfection is Oppression, Internalized

"Oh, by the way, I'll go to India with you, mum. But! I'm not going to Bombay, only to Goa. I just need to relax and unwind on the beach, and we can go see Papa's house. I can only give you eight days, and I wanna be back home for New Years."

I'm chatting on the phone with my mother, absent-mindedly scrubbing a pot that holds the burnt ends of some hodge podge dish I've ruined.

How am I going to spin this trip to my academic friends? Maybe I can shape it as an exotic getaway to a beach destination. Everyone was so jealous when Lydia and I went to Punta Cana earlier in the year. This trip could be the same type of getaway if I take the right photos and tell the right stories.

This practice of curating the right story has not always been a part of how I live. It is something I seem to have developed over what I call my "Swiss cheese years": the years between coming to Canada at 13 and leaving my parents home at 18. Of these years, I remember little to nothing. My therapists in the decades since have assured me that this is normal for brains that have experienced emotional and psychological trauma.

What I do remember is school, which was an incredible time for me. On my first day, I had no idea how to read a class schedule, or how to work the Dudley lock to my locker. I asked the girl whose locker was beside mine for help. She introduced herself as Valene, and told me that her name was to commemorate being born on Valentine's Day.

In high school, I excelled at academics. My teachers nourished and challenged me and helped me grow in ways immeasurable. My Grade 9 social studies teacher was the first person I ever told about there being trouble at home. I knocked at the teacher's lounge one morning, my eyes swollen from the fight with my mother.

"Can I speak to you for a minute, please Miss?"

"Is everything ok, Roselle?"

"I just need to talk to someone. Things are bad at home, and I don't know whom to talk to."

"Meet me in the chapel in 5 minutes, ok? I'm just finishing my breakfast."

In the eerily quiet chapel, I broke down, "I ran away from home, Miss."

"Where did you go?"

"I came here. To school."

School became my sanctuary from a worsening home space. My ragtag team of friends was a nerdy squad, most first generation immigrants, just like me, hailing from all over the world: India, Poland, Nigeria, the Philippines, Guatemala, Venezuela, Guyana, Iraq, to name a few. We spent lunch periods together, skipped classes together, ate at each others' homes, celebrated each others' cultural holidays, and together learned life's important answers about sex and love.

As I sobbed in the chapel, spilling home secrets for the first time, I realized that I couldn't tell any of my friends about what was happening at home. I feared that they would reject me for being bad and wouldn't believe me about how awful things were. So, throughout the Swiss cheese years, I mostly maintained the facade that I had a happy and healthy home life, just as I imagined my friends having.

As high school drew to a close, our tight little band of friends was heading off in many directions, most to post secondary, some to the trades and the workplace. We were frantically holding onto the last vestiges of a quickly dissipating childhood. By the time we were in Grade 13, a phenomenon now only known to a certain generation of Ontarians, we were bored out of our gourds and ready to get going into impending adulthood. We skipped school more than we should have. We went joyriding or daytime bowling or watched television in darkened basements. We ate fries in the school cafeteria and played round after round of card games. Our beloved teacher Mr. B would walk past us and laugh, "Get outta here, you scoundrels. You look miserable!"

It was the best, most languishing time. We'd seen each other grow from young adolescents to nearly adults. As graduation drew near, we held onto promises to be friends forever. It was with immense gravitas that we inscribed one anothers' yearbooks, writing long litanous paragraphs of promises and memories. I remember none of them, save for one. My friend Ana's words bothered me for a really long time.

Of all our friends, Ana, Lydia, Ritu and I were the closest knit. We'd had countless sleepovers at each others' homes, choreographed dances to emulate the East Compton Clovers, scared ourselves silly with late night horror films, taught each other about the mysterious mechanics of sex in the back of Ana's Corolla, jumped on her backyard trampoline a thousand times, and relished her mum's *moi moi*. Despite all of that, this is what Ana wrote in my yearbook:

> *Roselle. It's been wonderful to know*
> *you these past five years. I'm so grateful*
> *for our friendship. Life is going to take*
> *us into different directions. And I can't*
> *promise that we'll be friends after this.*
> *But I'm grateful for having known you*
> *through these five years of high school.*

Excuse me? I was pissed. Ana's words read as if she was throwing out our friendship and had no intention of remaining friends forever, which was the plan. In hindsight, she was right. We didn't remain friends forever. We didn't even keep in touch past a year into our post-high school lives. Every so often I'd hear from her, or Lydia would try and create a reunion, but the magic of our high school years was gone. Our lives had diverged.

Early on in high school, I'd become fast friends with Ritu. We both came from Indian families, albeit from different religio-cultural communities. Our friendship felt easy and familiar. I think we understood each other at a foundational level. Ritu was mischievous and hilarious, an exceptional dancer and full of optimism. So full of optimism in fact, that she even founded our high school's Hope Club. I'm not entirely certain what the purpose of the club was, but we met regularly and made poster boards about hope that we hung up around the school. I think we may have run fundraisers for global disaster relief. I don't think we raised very much money, but we had fun. I did say we were nerdy, right?

Ritu and I had a spectacular falling out somewhere between meeting and graduation. I have no recollection of what the spat was about. I probably did or said something hurtful, or self righteous, and then dug my heels in. There was probably a strongly worded letter in there somewhere, too. For my birthday that year, Ritu had curated a number of presents in a box for me. Our spat occurred just prior to me turning 16, and she gave me the box of presents despite our fight because she'd already made it. Inside the box was a flower vase, a number of other treasures, and a cassette tape.

I hit play on the black double tape deck in my bedroom and Ritu's voice filled the space. I can't recall everything she said, but the part that remains with me even these many years later is where she accused me of maintaining a veneer of perfection, of pretending that I came from the perfect family where we had no problems and had figured out superhuman ways of being in the world and with one another. She said that my perfect persona made it really difficult for her to trust me with her vulnerabilities.

I listened to the entirety of Ritu's tape that day, and then hit record to drown it out with white noise. Her words had pierced something deep in me. How *dare* she suggest that I was pretending that my family was perfect. They *were* perfect! *We* were perfect!

Though Ritu and I found some semblance of equilibrium a few months after our falling out, we never recovered.

✳

My first year of university in that bucolic Southern Ontario town had me paired with a stranger who would become one of my dearest friends. Donna and I got along like gangbusters before we even met in person that September. We had friends in common, ideas to share after late nights out, and ways of seeing the world that were both complementary and contradictory. Donna teased me about my love of old country music. I loved her over-preparedness and her enormous Tupperware container of first aid items, which I don't think she ever used! For nearly a decade, even after I transferred schools, Donna and I were the very best of friends.

A few years into our friendship, while I was in the midst of a dalliance with depression, Donna visited me in my tiny gerbil-y studio.

"Roselle, when we first met, you were the bravest person I'd ever known. You used to jump in with both feet and take chances. I hope you remember that part of yourself again."

She'd brought with her two delightful white stoneware ramekins as a gift. They were an absolute luxury for a graduate student whose entire collection of housewares was thrifted. Over the years, one of those ramekins has gotten lost, but the other one remains a precious part of my kitchen: a reminder to remember who I am, and the cherished friendship that sought to pull me out from my dark spaces.

In the year that I was slated to move to Calgary, Donna was due to get married to the love of her life. I was beyond excited to be her maid of honour. I'm not entirely certain what went wrong, but at the intersection of me writing a master's thesis and her planning a wedding was a collision waiting to happen. In the face of the friction in our friendship, my perfectionism reared its dual heads of righteousness and inflexibility. Instead of having a vulnerable and painful conversation with my beloved friend, I pulled a ripcord and ran away. My inability to bend caused me to pull out of Donna's wedding and shatter a friendship that had meant so much to me.

Pride kept me from reconnecting, but years later, I was grateful when Donna reached out. We would reconnect, but the friendship never returned to its original shape.

✱

In the early aughts, there was a great line in the HBO show *The Wire*, where Marla Daniels tells her spouse that a tree that won't bend will break. Lieutenant Cedric Daniels responds, "Bend too far, you're already broken."[1]

In these friendships that I've lost over the years, I wasn't a tree willing to bend. I wasn't willing to share my vulnerability, my heart, my sorrow, my fears. What resulted was the breaking of incredible bonds that weren't meant to sustain the illusion of perfection. What I have learned from these friendships that fell to neglect, rupture, and disrepair, is that I owe the benefit of trust to my relationships. That in order for me to find healing from the cognitive dissonance of mistrust, I would need to trust myself first, and trust that my dear ones will have space to hold me. Like the high school teacher who made me feel

1   The Wire. 2002. Season 5, Episode 10, "-30-." Directed by Clark Johnson. Aired March 9, 2008 on HBO.

safe in that school chapel those many years ago. I don't know how that story wraps up, Swiss cheese brain and all. What I do know is that anytime I encounter a chapel, I feel the same peace I felt as a young teenager, thanks to the memory of a teacher's safe presence.

One of the largest and earliest poison pills that I had swallowed in my younger years was the knowledge that I had to maintain the illusion of a perfect family to all external parties. I was to do this at all costs because outsiders were never to be trusted, lest they be vying to take advantage of me. That poison has permeated every relationship, and continues to be one for which I have to self-administer a regular antidote. It has sown seeds of doubt and distrust, not only in those around me, but most viciously, also in myself.

My belief in the correctness of what I'd been taught to believe about not trusting anyone outside our family was incongruent with the basic building blocks of good relations. Holding fast to this false set of ideas about trust in others meant that I sacrificed connection to myself and others in order to maintain the congruence of only trusting the people who'd perpetuated harm on me.

All of this would not be revealed to me for a long time though. For now, I am still heavily invested in the charade, committed to telling the right story to my academic friends about why I'm going to spend the break between semesters in Goa with my family.

✺

My mother is overjoyed that I'm going to India with her. She agrees quickly to my condition of only going to Goa. Now I need to lay the groundwork with my peers about why I won't be around for the holidays.

None of my graduate school friends, save for my pal Amit, knows that I was born in Bombay. I make sure to keep details about childhood vague enough to obfuscate any questions or suspicion of "otherness." I've become really practiced at this over the last few years. My name is Iberian enough that most folks don't immediately assume an Indian origin, and if the conversation ever goes deep enough that my heritage is enquired after, I make up some awkward response about being Indian, but of Portuguese descent.

Moving away from home after high school meant an opportunity for reinvention. This was an opportunity that I snagged in an attempt to get as far away from what I was running away from. In this reinvention, I wanted to fit in. I wanted to be like all the other Canadian girls. I wanted to engage in voracious drinking, Columbia windbreakers, and backpacking trips to find myself. In order to do that, I'd have to run away from my tethers to the old versions of me, to the old places. During that first year of university, when I had to take my mother to the airport, a dorm-mate chided me for having to miss out on a dorm party, "In this country, we don't bend to the whims of our parents. Just tell them to take a cab."

I wanted to explain to her the ties of filial piety that bound me, but every plausible response seemed ineffective. Instead, I internalized her sneer as truth, solidifying for me the notion that in order to fit in with my peers, I'd need to erase those tangled ties to that which made me "other."

Now on the cusp of this trip to Goa, I am half a decade into my reinvented self. The lie has taken hold, and I do not care for the times when my two worlds, with the carefully curated division between them, threaten to collide. So, I must now go about laying the groundwork to keep them safely apart.

"I just need a getaway," I tell my friends. "I need to lie on a beach and unwind. My parents have a villa in Goa, so I'm just going to go relax there!"

I will continue the nonchalant myth maintenance even during my trip to Goa, when in an email to one friend, who asks what I'm reading on the beach, I write, "I've got a couple books to read that are part of my academic bibliography, but instead I've gotten sidetracked by the love letters exchanged between Ginsburg and Kerouac. Be still my beating heart, those men had magic in words!"

Save for the part about the reading material, because I would actually be reading Chuck Klosterman's *Sex, Drugs, and Cocoa Puffs*, mostly because the title antagonized my mother, no individual piece of what I share is untrue, per se. My parents *do* have a villa on the beach in Goa. And, after my first semester of graduate school, I *do* need to unwind, and the beach *is* the perfect place to do that. What I omit is everything else: the real reason for the trip, about the house, my inheritance, or my Papa.

My peer group doesn't seem to have to worry about inheritances in old countries, or ties to places and foods and accents that are often reduced to cultural punchlines, or sneered at from the pedestal of Western cultural superiority. I am ashamed and embarrassed that I have these tethers, these constant signifiers of my otherness.

Over the years of trying to fit in, I have learned that if I tell the story just right, conceal enough about me to only share the bits that reflect the other person's life, then maybe I won't be seen as an outsider. I have become adept at shaping myself to fit into an imagined version of

who I need to be in order to be pleasing enough to the group into which I wished to fit. I have built a thick wall between my worlds: the one I am tethered to through my roots, and the one to which I desperately wish to belong.

It will be years before I realize that the high price of building a life around perfectionism and people-pleasing, is the heartbreaking grief of a life that is deeply invested in perpetual self-betrayal.

Get Lost

"Where are you from?"

I'm en route to India, and the aunty sitting a seat away from me on the flight from London to Delhi has been looking for a way to engage me for the last four hours. I've been curled up in my window seat, willing myself to be as invisible as possible, and grateful for the empty seat between us. At meal service, when I finally take off the headphones, she finds her entrypoint.

"Toronto," I respond, knowing what she is actually asking and wanting to be obstinate about giving in.

"Where are you going?" she presses on.

"Goa." My response is clipped. I hope she gets the cue that I am not really keen on chatting. She does not.

"Oh, that's where we're headed too! It's my dad and mom's sixtieth wedding anniversary, and our whole family is coming in from all over. Two of my brothers are in Australia, so they're coming with their wives and kids. My elder sister and I are in London, so our whole gang is on this flight. We're eleven of us. My other sister is coming from Toronto with her boys. I've been to Toronto many times. They're in Scarborough. Whereabouts are you from?"

Well, I guess we're chatting. I tell her that I grew up in Mississauga but that I now live in downtown Toronto.

"Oh, you must have been born there, huh?" Her English is a lilting combination of her original Indian accent, peppered with a British finish over time.

"Mmhmm."

I don't want to lie to this random aunty but I also have no interest in discussing the circumnavigation of my life story.

At the Delhi airport, aunty and her eleventeen family members run into their entire jing bang from Canada and Australia. There is joy and laughter, and I feel like the Grinch. Their mirth grates on my nerves.

I have purposely booked a flight directly from Delhi right to Goa, so I can avoid going through Bombay. I haven't been back there in a decade, and I have no interest in even landing in the city of my birth. The merriment of this Goan family seems to be a personal attack on me: an affront to all desire to shun my roots.

In the departure lounge, as we wait for our flight, aunty drags me back to her clan.

"Look. She's Goan too. From Toronto! Where in Goa are you going? We're from the south. We're going to Margao."

"My family's from the north," I feel trapped into giving details. "We're from Bardez side, but my parents have a house in the south, so I'm going to Margao too."

Aunty's brother pipes in, "Oh! Smashing! Maybe we can share a cab when we land."

Judgement over his use of Aussie slang distracts me from his generosity.

"Who does he think he's fooling? Everyone knows he's Indian!" I kvetch to myself, my own hypocrisy notwithstanding.

"Thanks, Uncle. My mom is picking me up at the airport in Goa."

"Oh, good! Then she can give us a ride!"

His corny uncle joke elicits both laughter and shushes from his family. I go back to reading Klosterman.

The Delhi heat is overwhelming even inside the allegedly air conditioned departure terminal. George Jones sings "He Stopped Loving Her Today" in my earphones. Uninvited fat tears threaten to melt out of my eyes. I've forgotten that I love this song. I only ever listen to it in secret because loving old country music has no place in my current carefully constructed life. The Possum's lyrics remind me of the pieces of myself that I've sacrificed. I feel the inexplicable loss of those pieces so acutely in this moment, and I can't sit for too long in this dissonant space.

My heart beating in my ears becomes deafening. My entire being feels buzzy. George fades out and I can no longer hear anything over the rushing sensation in my ears. There isn't enough oxygen in this airport. I have to take a walk. Maybe eating something will help.

I approach the snack shop counter, keeping my Canadian passport visible so all who encounter it will know where I'm from.

"Madam, *aapko kyaa chaiyye?*"

(Madam, what do you want?)

Annoyed that the shop attendant assumes that I'd

understand him, I tell him that I don't understand what he's saying even though I do.

He reiterates in English, and I walk away with a chutney and cheese sandwich and a Limca.

Being in this place is discordant with the persona of myself that I've become comfortable living as these last few years. Being here feels like an affront to that persona, and I can feel the slimy tendrils of incongruence all over me as I walk away from the food stall.

I toss the sandwich, mostly uneaten, in a nearby dustbin. Nowhere seems like a safe space to land. I curse my decision to come back to this bloody country.

The ceaseless roaring and buzzing in my ears is familiar.

It was after church, a monsoon day. Mama drove us to the Bandra fish market on the scooter, a canary yellow Honda Kinetic, on which I always thought she felt most free. We parked the bike in the bike lot, amongst what seemed like a thousand others. I was wearing my gumboots and a yellow raincoat, a translucent flimsy thing perfect for the warm Bombay drizzle.

As we arrived at the market, covered in corrugated metal sheets and black tarps, the raindrops became simultaneously amplified and also woven into the cacophony of the market. I wiggled uncomfortably in my now too-warm raincoat as we wound our way through long rows of *machchiwalis*, fishmongers. On their platforms, each one squatted over the day's bounty. The smell of fresh fish enveloped me: some small, perfect for frying, and some bigger than me. I was hoping for pomfrets, my favourite. Or maybe *bangdas*, so Achie could stuff them with *rechaad masala.* Tangy, crispy perfection for a rainy Sunday lunch.

Old Chimbai aunties in their *kashtiis* squatted and gutted the fish, preparing them for sale. I loved being at the *machchi* bazaar, surrounded by Marathi, my paternal tongue, and a language of the Konkan coast. My nana Cecilia was of *Koli* people, a tribe indigenous to this land and sea, from long before anyone had come to the subcontinent. Nana was born, like me, on the ocean's edge, at the same maternity clinic even! Also like me, she was salty, not tender. I don't recall her being particularly nice to me, though she did affectionately call me *tombola*, and made a mean oxtail curry. I suppose that's another thing we shared: showing our love through food.

Nana was what one might describe as a handsome woman. Her high cheeks and plump lips created stark features on her deep brown skin. I'm grateful to have inherited those cheeks and her wicked sense of style. I loved her giant translucent sunglasses, donned on her way to church every day. She sacrificed neither piety nor vanity. Years later, when Alzheimer's had stolen most of her mind, Nana would come to live with us, but this trip to the fish market was years before all that.

I don't think Mama liked the fish market. These were not her people. This was not her native tongue. Looking back now, I think Mama felt perpetually an outsider in Bandra, a place to which she'd moved after getting married, a place to which I belonged by mere virtue of being born to the right lineage, in the right place.

I got chatting with one of the *machchiwalis* in Marathi. I imagine now that this dawdling annoyed my mother. There was an errand to be done, and the sooner we were done with it, the sooner she'd be out of the infernal chaos of yelling, puddles of water and fish guts, and nasal assault. I looked up from my conversation to find Mama gone. Oops!

I couldn't see her anywhere. I knew which fish ladies Mama liked best, and knew that she'd make her way to them one after another, so I followed her imagined footsteps and made my way through the market, dodging bodies and other shoppers with their big plastic baskets.

"Aunty, *tumhi majya aiila pahile ka?*"

(Aunty, have you seen my mother?)

"*Nahi, nahi*, baby."

(No, no, baby.)

None of the three *machchiwalis* could recall seeing her. Panic started to set in. I had looked everywhere, retracing my steps a few times over.

No Mama anywhere.

Ok, think Roselle. Miss Manju's house is close by. You can walk home, if you need to, I coached myself.

But that would make Mama angry.

OK, I'll go back to where we parked the scooter, and wait there. I figured that would be the best course of action, and I could wait there for the inevitable onslaught of anger that I feared my dilly dalliance would be met with. I exited the market. It was nice to be outside again, cooler and less sticky in my raincoat. I wound my way through the other scooters.

I waited at our bike for what could have been minutes or hours anticipating, scared. Something bad must have happened to Mama. If not, something bad was about to happen to me! What was I going to tell Mama? I didn't mean to get lost, I swear.

Aha! There she was, winding her way towards me.

"Mama!" I was elated to see her finally.

She clipped her shopping to the scooter's hook.

"Mama! What happened?! I looked for you every-where!!"

She looked at me as though she'd just noticed me.

"Mama! I got lost, and you were gone. I went to all the *machchiwalis*, but you weren't there!"

"What do you mean? You weren't with me?"

"No! Mama! I came here and stood to wait for you. I couldn't find you anywhere, so I came here. I waited here."

"Oh, I thought you were behind me."

I had been lost and terrified. I had scrambled through fish guts and the sticky humid market. Half crying in the rain, trying to tell her of my harrowing journey, I realized Mama hadn't even noticed that I had been lost. In her mind, there was nothing to make a fuss of because nothing had happened. We got back on the bike and went home, as if nothing had.

That day, I learned that my perception of an event wasn't necessarily the version of events that everyone around me held. My emotions have always run deep and strong, and getting lost in the fish market created tidal waves that bashed against my wounds of being unwant-ed. It would take me years to learn that though my feel-ings weren't necessarily shared by those around me, they weren't any less true.

My experience at the fish market also taught me that as long as I was present at the start and end of something, the primary adult in my life didn't really care what I did in the middle. It became my very favourite thing to take to getting lost in that space between.

✴

The year I was in 2nd standard, my friend Andrea lived near the Bandra bazaar. The bazaar was in the opposite direction of my house, but that year, I started walking Andrea home after school. Andrea and I would sing Michael Jackson songs, making sure to memorize the lyrics the next time we heard the song so that we could sing it better! Jackson's "Black or White" was a favourite.

After dropping Andrea off, I'd dawdle through the bazaar, past a house that I knew I was never supposed to go to, though I wasn't sure why. The grownups only spoke of it in whispers, in a code I didn't understand. Years later I would learn that it was my paternal grandfather's ancestral home. Papa Leo had been disowned upon getting his girlfriend Cecelia, my nana, pregnant when they were both teenagers. The pregnancy itself was shameful enough, but that the girl was from a lower caste, a tribal class, that would not abide.

I felt naughty sneaking past that house, but I *needed* to know what was in there. Who were these people? I peeked inside once or twice, but I had to keep moving for fear of being seen. I wish now that I had knocked on the door, maybe asked for a cup of water as a ruse to enter. Everyone connected to the myth of that home, that rupture, that storyline, is now gone. I wonder if the house even remains.

Winding my way through the bazaar, and back across Hill Road, I'd sometimes nick a few boiled peanuts from the cart parked across the church. Then I'd make my way home. Sometimes Achie would chastise me for coming home late:

"What if Mama was home already? You'll get a pasting!"

I knew though, that pastings were inevitable, so why bother trying to stave them off? Also, Mama was usually home only after five o'clock, so as long as I was home before then, she would never even know.

In the space between the two times in a day when my mother cared about where I was, I filled my life with brave adventures. I'd wind down streets I'd never been down before. I'd make up rules for the particular day: one day, only right turns, another day only roads named after saints. Along the way, I made friends with all sorts of people, sometimes other children, but mostly with adults whom the world didn't seem to value.

I learned that there are so very many ways to get back home.

✸

The year I was in the 3rd standard, I'd walk home from school down St. Paul's Road and wave at an uncle on his fourth floor balcony. He was always there in the afternoons.

"Hello uncle."

"Hello, baby! How was school today?" He'd wave back down to me.

Over time we became good friends, always separated by four floors. I learned that he had no legs, so that's why he never came down. He'd ask about what I'd learned in school, and sometimes he'd quiz me on my times tables. I was good at maths and loved his quizzes, hollering the answers up to him from the ground! One day he invited me up to his flat, and I ran up.

"Baby, someone gave me this chocolate, but you know I have diabetes so I can't eat it. I saved it for you." He handed me a bright yellow chocolate bar. "I was looking for you today."

I hugged him, and ran home elated. When Mama got home that evening, I showed her my treasure.

"Look at what uncle gave me, Mama!"

"Who is this uncle?"

"He lives in that yellow building, you know, on St. Paul's Road. He lives on the fourth floor. He doesn't have any legs! He's nice, Mama."

"You can't eat this. It could be poisoned," she said and got into the shower. The conversation was over.

I knew that trying to convince Mama would be futile. I had to throw away the chocolate. Sobbing, I handed it to Achie in the kitchen.

"Mama…said…I have to throw…this…out."

I couldn't bear to put it in the dustbin myself. After that, I took a different route home from school, ashamed of what I'd done to uncle's kind gift, embarrassed that I'd become friends with him when I wasn't supposed to, and deeply confused as to why. I was enraged at the unfairness of it all. Uncle would never poison a chocolate bar!

Later that year, I also had to throw away a lavender body wash gifted to me by an old aunty whom I met by the Chimbai *banya*, dawdling home from elocution classes at Betty Vincent's. I liked taking the inside roads by the sea shore, instead of the busier, but quicker, Perry Road that went straight home. The old aunty by the *banya* had wild hair, matted in places, and mostly white. We became friends because she said something while I was walking past her one day, and I responded. She hadn't been speaking to me, and I learned later that she spoke out loud to herself a lot, but rarely did anyone stop to respond to her. When I did, she perked up as if snapping out of a reverie. We struck up a chat. She showed me the little cart in which she kept all her things. People living on the street were commonplace in Bombay, and I thought nothing of her being unhoused.

Every Wednesday evening, I'd head to elocution

lessons.

"She sells seashells by the seashore." Ten times fast.

"Vuh is for vee." I bit my lip as I'd been taught.

"Wuh is for double you." I made an O with my lips to rush the air out my mouth.

"Vuh. Wuh. Vuh. Wuh. Vuh. Wuh."

An hour or two of aspiration and breathing exercises, some recitation practice, and then I'd wind my way home through the back streets, to visit my old friend, who was usually in the same vicinity.

One evening, she seemed really excited to see me.

"Baby! Baby! Good, I was waiting for you. Come see! I kept something for you."

She gave me a half bottle of lavender-scented body wash that she'd saved for me.

"I can't use this baby. Where am I going to have a bath! You take it. It smells so nice."

"*Chee chee*! That's filthy," Mama said when I got home with my gift.

I was forced to pour it down the drain. Apparently I wasn't allowed to take things from beggars.

I later lied to the old aunty and told her that I had used the soap and that I liked it a lot. For weeks after, she inquired about it, and every time, I felt so much shame for discarding her present. A few weeks later, I asked Achie if I could take the aunty a Christmas plate, and I got to repay her kindness with some sweets, a couple *pao*, and whatever else Achie packed into the tinfoil-wrapped packet.

The aunty laid her hands on the sides of my head and blessed me. After that, I learned to keep to myself whatever I found while getting lost. It hurt too much to reveal what I treasured only to have to toss it in the dustbin, and have my friends' intentions maligned.

✱

The human amygdala doesn't know the difference between fear rooted in unsafety and fear rooted in discomfort. Its goal is to keep us safe, and more often than not, it codes discomfort with a safety signal gone awry. This is what makes it so difficult for us to trust people unlike ourselves, to receive kindness without suspecting an underlying motive, to explore ideas outside of our echo chambers.

There's a lot of fear that the world outside may be scary. Hushed tones abound about the dangers that lurk in unknown spaces. Fear dictates that things not known may be poisonous and filthy. It is easy to waste generations perpetuating those fears. Fear turns protection into protectionism. Being willing to lean into the discomfort of being a little lost can yield joy, and delight, and gifts, and knowledge.

When fear floods my amygdala, my first instinct is to flee. To run and hide from whatever danger, real or imagined, is imminent. This desire to run away is thwarted at the moment by the fact that I have a literal flight to board in a while. I have nowhere to flee to as the buzzing in my body crescendos in the sweltering Delhi airport.

Having tossed my uneaten sandwich and Limca, I find another seat in which to wait for the flight to Goa, making sure to sit farther away from the merry family. I really resent their camaraderie.

The plane ride from Delhi to Goa is turbulent, both physically and emotionally, and I am relieved to step off the plane into the Goan sunshine.

The damp air and ocean breeze rush up to me, enveloping me in an embrace reminiscent of an old friend whom you haven't seen for years and who loves you regardless of the time that passes between visits.

My eyes become misty. The gushing in my ears is replaced by the sound- and scent-scapes of memories long buried. For the first time in what feels like forever, I take an enormous, lung-expanding breath.

There are blessings to be received in the space between being at home and coming back home.

Inheritances and Heirs

"What does one wear to visit one's ancestral home? Is it like church? Will the ancestors be there, judging me?"

I'm chatting out loud to nobody in particular, parading my sartorial choices like I'm on *What Not to Wear*, as if some judgy TV personalities will be critiquing my fashion choices. This mundanity is taking up all my brain space on the morning of the impending visit to Papa's family estate, the whole reason for this trip to India.

"Perhaps a cute frock?" I slip on my favourite sandals, and pose in the mirror.

"No no," my mother vetoes from her perch on the couch. "The place has thorns. Wear proper shoes."

Finally, I put on a fancy tank top and linen shorts, and throw my trusty scarf around my neck. I hope the ancestors appreciate Club Monaco. Oversized sunglasses and statement earrings are added to the ensemble because I would rather be dead than sans accessories.

The drive to the house takes a couple of hours. En route, I think about Lydia's suggestion to pick up a token from the house so that even if it gets sold, I'll have a piece of it to remember my Papa by. I haven't shared this idea with anyone. I fear being jeered at for my sentimentality. Naturally tender-hearted, years of being mocked have taught me to bury it under layers of sarcasm, eye rolls, and not caring. I don't dare expose this plan to contempt.

We enter the village of Ucassaim, Papa's ancestral village, and my mother gasps as she spots the local church. A bright white building with vibrant blue trim and a statue of the Virgin Mary out front, her arms outstretched, as if to say, "Welcome home."

"I haven't seen this church in so many years. It looks so nice," my mother says, her eyes lost in a memory.

The deeper we get into the village, the narrower the roadways become, until they are no more than a couple of feet wider than the van we are in. Roadways from a time before cars are lined on either side by red stone walls and lush greenery. The van pulls over at one point to let a bicycle pass in the opposite direction.

My thighs are attached to the plastic seats, and I am getting impatient. I don't think I ask it out loud, but I am definitely wondering if we're there yet. Village life seems relaxed: women hanging laundry in the yard, small children chasing a ball down the road with a stick, men walking unhurriedly. I wonder where they're going.

Fragments of lives I'll never touch.

The van driver seems uncertain about where we are going.

"Are we lost?"

My mother stops the van, and asks some local women:

"Aunty, aunty. *Zaano*, Menezes *ghar qwhi hahn?*"

She asks if the aunties know where the old Menezes house is. In Konkani, she tells them that no one has lived there for a long time. They don't know. My mother offers another clue: the family supplied bread to the village. They were the local bakery many years ago. That tidbit seems to trigger something in the women.

"*Angasor hanh. Phude voss.*"

(It's right here. Go straight.)

Equipped with classic old-world directions, we head off once more.

We pull up to what seems, to my unaccustomed eyes, to be the middle of the brush. The roadway has ended and given way to a leaf-littered ground with a crumbling red stone wall nearby and overgrown trees all around.

"There!"

My mother points to a slight break in the brush, and I see the once-majestic old colonial-style bungalow. The stone pillars and stairs of the *balcão* still stand, though the verandah roof is missing. The chalk-white exterior walls are still bright, though decades of disrepair show in the foundation and falling eavestroughs. Vines have taken over and weave in and out of the shuttered windows. I imagine someone taking great pride in lovingly painting the shutters. The house hasn't been lived in or attended to for nearly 80 years. Still, the teal windows point to a yesteryear of care.

"I remember that window," I squeal. "Mom! Re-member you told me not to go inside because there were snakes inside?"

I have a memory, faded like the colour of the windows I so desperately wanted to look through.

My mother chuckles. "You must have been three or four when we came here. You remember everything."

I get no confirmation on the snakes. Were they real? Are they gone? Is it safe for me to peer in now?

We walk the perimeter of the house. The overgrown garden still holds its mango trees. My mother points to them, lamenting the lost wealth of the family.

"See? We had such beautiful trees. We were the *capitãos* of the village."

Her tone is mournful for all that has been lost. She waves at the now-crumbling, once-grand estate in front of us. "I came here when I was seventeen, right after I sat for my SSC exams. Just before I went to the convent. I was so angry with Papa. We grew up in that two-room tenement in *Dhobi Talao*, when we could have had all this?"

To a teenager who'd grown up in abject poverty, it was unfathomable that she could have had access to such largesse. For a moment, right before my eyes, my mother morphs into that seventeen-year-old version of herself, yearning and resentful.

✳

Papa's first wife died in mysterious circumstances. Family whispers suggest that she took her life in the very house that now stands in front of me, unable to endure her broken heart at the death of her infant son. Widowed, with three daughters aged 8 to 18, Papa was compelled to marry again, this time to a woman half his age and barely 5 years older than his eldest daughter.

My maternal grandmother, Ana Paula by birth but Omai to us all, was Papa's second wife. Brought from Goa to the bustling metropolis of Bombay to marry Papa, she was a Konkani-speaking woman in her early twenties. She never returned to her Goan village or to her mother's house.

Omai's life had been painted by both privilege and pain. The first-born of a high-class family, she was forced to fend for her siblings at the age of 18 upon the death of her own father, a policeman who died in the line of duty. Marrying a high-born widower in Bombay was one way for her to ensure that her mother and family would be cared for.

Omai would bear six living children, struggle to make ends meet her whole married life, and die almost exactly nine months before I entered the world. I like to imagine that in the interstitial space between this life and the great beyond, her spirit and mine passed each other and nodded in recognition, like two actors, one exiting while the other is cued for her onstage entrance.

Omai was Papa's second choice: a second wife in a marriage born of necessity and survival.

While I'm no expert on the epigenetics of inter-generational trauma, I am given to understand that our current leading knowledge in the field would suggest that the impact of trauma runs on the matrilineal line, like a DNA-altering steam engine, doling out the impacts of trauma at regular stops from mother to daughter to grand-daughter. The parental loss, poverty, and choicelessness that Omai experienced would leave permanent marks on my mother, Omai's second daughter.

In traditional Goan families, a first daughter is an honour and a burden. A burden because she is raised to benefit the family she will marry into. However, raising her well means upholding family honour through her marrying and carrying on tradition.

A second daughter in an already impoverished family, is just a burden. And so, when my mother was but a few weeks old, well-off relatives from Goa arrived to take her off my grandparents' hands. Papa and Omai already had two boys and a girl in addition to Papa's first three daughters, and the family was struggling to make ends meet. My mother's adoption, a kind mercy of sorts, meant that at merely a few weeks old, she was spirited off from my grandparents' home in Bombay, to Goa, where she lived for the better part of her first year before Omai couldn't bear the idea of having abandoned her second daughter, and retrieved her.

Though my mother was returned to her natal home within months of having been sent away, abandonment and anxious attachment have been marked into her skin.

The second wife's second daughter would never again feel like anybody's first choice.

Having experienced a life of poverty and deeply entrenched shame, my mother at the young age of 17, would choose to remove herself from being a burden on her family by joining a convent to become a nun. Her first cousin, Sr. Clementina, was already a nun at Auxelium Convent, run by the Salesian Order.

There is an old adage that runs deep in big Goan Catholic families: you have one son to carry your name and another to carry on the work of the Lord. Each big Goan family of yesteryear was bound to have at least one or two members join a religious order. Not only did this increase a family's bounty heaven-side, but it also served to lessen the burden of finding good marriages for them here on Earth.

My mother's time in the convent was short-lived, punctuated by night terrors and anxieties that made her unfit for a life of self-reflection, solitude, and piety. Sent back from her first choice of escape, shame likely crept its way into the very fabric of who my mother would become in this world.

A few years after her stint at religious life, she met my father at a party. I don't think it was anything akin to attraction that drew her to him. My guess is that she was more attracted to his social standing, his bravado, his earning potential, and how far from her own life, and shame, he could take her if they married.

✳

"Come on, let's go." My mother snaps out of her reverie, apparently surprised and annoyed to still be in this place.

"Let's take a picture," I say in true millennial fashion.

As we walk to the van, I remember my quest for the day: "Go ahead, I'll be right back. I'll meet you at the van. Two minutes."

I run back to the house and search around frantically. A leaf to tuck into a book? No, too fragile. The rubble on the ground isn't substantial enough. Dammit, I should have planned better. The rushing sound in my ears is back as I hear my mother yell for me from the van: "Come on! We're going!"

Aha! I have found just the thing. Tucked under some debris and dead leaves, a palm-sized piece of a red roof tile. Jagged-edged, but solid. I grab it and use my scarf to wipe off the wet moss on its underside. From my satchel, I grab a plastic bag that I brought just in case. Wrapping the tile in the plastic bag, I hurry back to the van, zipping my satchel.

"What were you doing?"

"I just wanted to look at something."

I'm not ready to talk about what I've done or why. I don't think I even fully understand it myself.

Ties that Bind

The van ride away from Papa's house finds me surreptitiously clutching at the piece of tile safely tucked into my satchel, as if to assure myself that it is real. I did it. I found my own piece of the ancestral home to link me to generations of people who make up my bloodline. To link me to Papa, and the gifts he left me.

As we zoom away from the house, I whisper a prayer I've uttered as far back as my memory goes.

> *Deo bori rath*
> *Amkam somestank deo dhiu*
> *Asleleank bolaiki*
> *Meleleank sorg kurpecheo*
> *Bessaum*
> *Gal saiba*
> *Amen.*

This old Konkani prayer sits on my lips every night, even though my cords to the language and the faith have unwound over time and place. Now, if I don't recite it fast enough or at the right cadence, from a part of my brain that remains four years old, my mind will trip over the words. As I trace the outline of the baked red clay in my lap and whisper the words, I'm grateful to have learned it.

Papa taught me the prayer. Diligently. Deliberately.

"*Sheek*," he'd say to me.

(Learn)

He encouraged me to learn everything I could, and to be curious about the world. If my mission in life has become one of an eternal student, it was probably infused into me by him.

After saying daily prayers together, Papa would bless me. Every night after the family Rosary, even in his latter days, when he couldn't join us in the living room to pray, I'd go to his bed for the first blessing. He was my most special person, and what he blessed me with has yielded a life I hope he'd be proud of.

As a four-year-old, I didn't know to cherish what would be our short time together. I didn't know then that my final memory of him would be the last one I'd ever have the chance to make. I'd just run home from school, and was greeted at the door by my mother's elder sister. She used her sweet, happy voice for me, but I could tell she didn't feel that way. I passed Papa's bedroom. He was lying on the bed in a black suit, wads of cotton stuffed in his nose.

"Aunty, why is there cotton in Papa's nose? Does he have a cold?"

Sometimes when I had a stuffy nose, Achie would soak cotton balls with a bit of Vicks VapoRub and hold it to my nostrils. I hated the feeling of cotton on my nostrils and worried Papa wouldn't like it either.

A few nights before, there'd been a kerfuffle in the house. Papa had fallen and needed to be taken to the hospital. I heard the word "stroke," and when Mama and I went to the hospital, Papa seemed very weak. Even though it was difficult for him to speak, he still blessed me, haltingly, from his hospital bed.

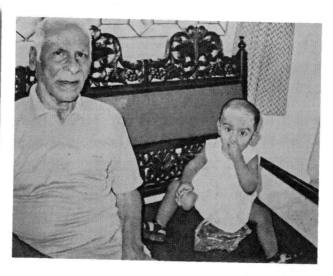

"No baby. It's ok. Papa is no more," my aunty assuaged my concern about the cotton in Papa's nose, trying to find the right words to euphemistically tell me that Papa was dead. Then she finally let her face get wet with tears.

I wore a red jumper when all the family came over. Papa lay in the hall of our flat, and we gathered around, crying and praying. I got to say a whole decade of the Rosary. I counted the beads carefully. I didn't understand why everyone was so sad, so I said my Hail Marys with extra care. Mama had arranged a bus to take us to the cemetery, to her family's burial plot.

We stood by the open grave, Papa's coffin draped in green, lowering into the earth, and Mama handed me a small pail filled with soil.

"Put it on the coffin."

I didn't understand, and asked my mother why we were throwing dirt at Papa?

"From dust we come, and to dust we will return," was all she said. I pretended to understand.

Papa was buried in a simple coffin. His gravesite, one I haven't returned to since that warm March afternoon in the late 1980s, is shared with Omai. It is far, far away from the Goan estate bequeathed to him by his wealthy family, the one that now lies in ruin, uninhabited these many decades later. Papa was the youngest of his line and the eldest of mine. With his death, save for this broken red roof tile in my satchel, all ties that I might have had to him are gone.

I fly back home to Toronto eight days after arriving in Goa, excited to show my friends photos of my alleged beach vacation, complete with the stereotypical photo of free-roaming cows that every traveler through India is compelled to take. I give no thought to whether to reveal anything about the house visit or the tile. There is no room in the world I yearn to fit into, for this version of me—the one tethered to my roots.

Before heading back to my studio in the city, I spend a few nights at my parents' home. My teenage bedroom is untouched, as if I am expected to return imminently, even though I haven't lived there in years. I value the familiarity of a comfortable place, even if it is one that only awaits an apparition of me.

Years earlier, my dad and I built a custom bookshelf for the family kitchen. Other than our love of country music, woodworking is probably the only interest he and

I shared. We both have mathematical minds, and love working with our hands. Using tools and measuring angles has always been a great way for us to spend quality time together, even if this did not happen too frequently. When my parents had their kitchen remodeled, they considered getting rid of the giant bookshelf that I'd been so proud of having a hand in building. At my request, they put the bookshelf in my room, so that I might someday take it to a home of my own.

The bookshelf in my teenage bedroom is laden with books and mementos. It is here, amongst baskets of treasures, that I think to safekeep the little piece of red tile from Papa's house. The bookcase is filled with things I plan to someday take to my own home, when I find a permanent landing space beyond the life of studenthood. I carefully place the tile, wrapped in its plastic bag for safekeeping among my journals, yearbooks, photos from trips, and other precious things. It would take up no space in my city apartment, but there is no context for it in my hipster academic life, untethered from the past. I don't need a constant reminder of my incongruous identity.

The visit to Papa's house, and the talisman in my care, root me to where I come from, and tap into a deep yearning within me. A yearning for wholeness that I didn't know I'd been in search of, possibly my entire life. The piece of tile, dormant in that cupboard, beats silently like a tell tale heart.

Whenever I visit my parents, I take it out, just to make sure it is real. Over the next few years, the beating of the buried heart becomes louder, demanding to be heard. What it seems to long for is a bridging of the worlds between which I've built a chasm: on one shore, my roots and history, and on the other, the world in which I am building a life, finding purpose and joy and meaning.

✳

A year after returning from Goa, I apply to doctoral programs, with the intention of continuing my graduate research on the impacts that American Evangelical communities have on policy-making that police the sexuality and gender expression of marginalized groups. I accept an offer to join a doctoral program in Calgary, where I know not a soul.

"Why would you go there? They're not welcoming like us, you know."

I have no substantive response to these inquisitions, presented to me repeatedly from well-meaning loved ones. Alberta's reputation for being the Texas of Canada tickles the love of outlaw country music baked deep in my heart. The prospect of finding a cowboy of my own feels thrilling. Also, the adventure presents an opportunity for yet another reinvention, allowing me to explore who I can become in this third place, away from my places of birth and of discordant, maladaptive, growth.

A few weeks after packing my Toronto life into a few suitcases, I find myself in Calgary, with a whole new set of peers. Everything is foreign: the landscape, the people, perhaps even myself. Those first weeks also fill me with disillusionment at my proposed research project, and in a chat with a new classmate-turned-friend, I share my disengagement.

"I'm just not feeling my research, you know? It's not thrilling me. I don't know if I can do five years of this."

My friend listens to my kvetching, and then asks, "If there's one project you could do, what would it be? What would bring you joy?"

I think back to the trip to Goa, and the piece of tile from Papa's house. The semester after I came home from Goa, I was invited by a professor to attend a colloquium on the topic of Indian Christianity and the concepts of enculturation. For the very first time, I had found myself truly excited by an academic conversation. I had never considered the identity of my Indo-Catholic family and community as something worthy of inquiry within the academic ivory tower.

Between the trip back to Goa for the tile, and this colloquium, something within me became unleashed: a well of questions regarding my own identity, culture, history, and narrative. Telling my friend in Calgary about this transformation, I become impassioned and dynamic in my description of the hypothetical research I could do if I had the freedom to study anything. My body rocking back and forth as if the material were bursting forth from within my being.

"They'll never let me do that though. I can't switch my project now; they already admitted me based on my proposal. Also, I can't study my own people."

Studying one's own people is academically verboten because a researcher must always uphold the illusion of being an objective outsider, as if that is ever a thing.

"If you tell them exactly what you just told me, exactly how you told me, they will have a very hard time turning you down. I think you have something really beautiful here, my friend."

That night, heeding my friend's guidance, I stay awake for hours drafting a research proposal, fully expecting it to be rejected, and hoping fervently that it won't also result in me being kicked out of the doctoral program altogether.

Exhausted from an all-nighter, but buzzing from the exciting prospect of what might lie ahead, I call Lydia before heading into the office to pitch my zany idea to my supervisors. In a rush born of too much caffeine and just as much adrenaline, I fill her in.

In all our years of friendship, I have heard Lydia's voice crack only a handful of times. Signature stoicism be damned: "Roselle, this is the most powerful thing I've ever heard you talk about, and it makes so much sense for you to be the one to do this research and tell this story. This is the work you need to do."

That is all I need: for the person who has known me best to validate that I am onto something precious. What follows changes the course of my entire doctorate, and indeed my life: my supervisor and the department head approve my newly-drafted research proposal on the spot. In it, I detail a three-year-long, multi-sited, ethnographic inquiry into the identity construction of a community that sits in the interstitial spaces between religion and culture, place and time, myth and meaning.

If I am to ever stand a chance of building a purpose-driven, joy-filled, meaningful life outwards, this is the time for me to go inwards. It is time for me to explore the nooks and crannies of the ties that bind me to all of that which came before.

Trauma in a person,
decontextualized over time,
looks like personality.

Trauma in a family,
decontextualized over time,
looks like family traits.

Trauma in a people
decontextualized over time,
looks like culture.

—Resmaa Menakem
"Talk Easy with Sam Fragoso" Podcast, 2020

Rupture

2013

Of Old Cowboys and Fallen Heroes

I read the latest vodka-soaked email from my father.

"You are no longer our daughter, and you are no longer welcome in our home. Moreover, you should arrange to have 'your' belongings removed from our home within six months, after which I will be disposing of them."

I zero in on the incomprehensible words.

"You are no longer our daughter."

Is this for real?

"You are no longer welcome in our home."

I read it again, as if my comprehension of the written word has suddenly been upended.

I step away from my desk. What am I missing? Over the years, I've received many a vitriolic email from my father, but this one feels different. Uglier. More cruel.

I keep returning to my desk to re-read the email.

My dad's alcoholism has always been a part of our lives, but over the past few years, it has spiraled out of control, more often than not resulting in him penning long hateful missives to me and other family members and friends for perceived slights and disrespect.

So much of the story of my dad is now narrativized through my adult eyes. The truth is that I don't have very many memories, and I now realize that I barely knew anything about him to begin with. The youngest of his siblings, he was malnourished and mistreated, working for his father's bootlegging business from a young age. A high performance athlete with aspirations of a college scholarship, he was embittered about being pulled out of the 11th standard and put to work. He started smoking and drinking young, and in his late teens had been responsible for the death of his friend in a DUI situation, one he never fully explained.

After our move to Canada, my father's drinking took a prominent place in our home. He'd be gone for weeks to offshore oil fields in increasingly dangerous locales: Venezuela, Brunei, Algeria, Iraq. His brushes with danger and death became something we had to contend with when he was away. His cleaving to the bottle was something we dealt with when he was home.

Over the years, whiskey was replaced with vodka. It was easier to disguise how much vodka was in a glass topped off with water. The vodka bottles themselves were hidden in cabinets, in bins, in the dishwasher, in the laundry room. My mother would stop at the liquor store and buy vodka on her way home from work, and sneak it into dad's hiding places. We'd all pretend that this system worked.

When he was home, we structured our days around

his drinking schedule. Tuesdays, Thursdays, and the weekends were dad's regularly scheduled drinking days. Friends couldn't come over right before his drinking days because he'd be the most cranky then. Surely not *on* his drinking days, or on the day after either.

Be quiet, be gentle, don't listen to music too loudly, stay in your room, offer to feed him, offer to buy him more booze.

These were the rules.

Failure to adhere to the rules resulted in chaos.

✷

"Dad, please. Please, dad. It's too much. Christmas was completely ruined. You drank so much and it's so hard to pick you off the stairs when you fall. I'm scared you'll hit your head and be hurt. Please, dad, you need to stop drinking so much."

I sobbed, my pleas futile against the steely look in my father's eyes. One of his hands clenched in a fist, the other gripped the neck of a bottle he'd been unwilling to surrender to me. Suddenly the air got deadly still. Like a knife cutting through the air, into my heart, my father spat at me:

"Get away from me. *You're* the reason I drink."

It was just after New Year, and the holiday season had been one fraught with my father's binging, my mother's crying, my brother's withdrawal, and my perpetual attempt to fix everything. My father's outburst validated my deepest fears: that I was the reason he drank, and that he would stop were I a better person.

Jan 24, 2005

Today. It was today. A year ago today.

She couldn't stand by and watch the yelling.
Watch the screaming and the waving of the
bottle. The threats and the shouts were too
much. What was she to do? She may have been
twenty on the outside, but she was frightened
and five on the inside. Trembling,
she coaxed him into turning his wrath away
from her mother and onto her. Because she
knew she could handle it. She'd already made
up her mind about what to do.

As he screamed at her, she saw her mother
crumble in the corner, clutching the bottle of
whiskey - the one she wouldn't let him take
another sip from. This was his curse..the one
his father'd given to him. "Happy Birthday
son..here's your present - a life-fucking-long
membership to the world of alcoholism."

All she could think of as she dialled three little
digits was that she would never let that
curse reach her. Never. It would not become
her baggage. It would stop here here- - at

his generation. It would be buried with his body when he left this earth. The words tumbled out as the operator picked up on the other end: "911, what's your emergency?" She was sobbing and through her sobs, she died a little bit that day.

It broke her, and in many ways changed her forever.

She's very much like him in so many ways - her temper, her passion, her convictions, her heart.

She doesn't tell anyone about it. They never spoke of it again. They pretend like it never happened. But they both know it's there.

Like a giant bottle of whiskey hidden from sight in the cabinet, in the dishwasher, in the hutch. It's there. It's there but never spoken of.
Until now.
Now you've heard her story.
And maybe by telling you, she can let go of it a little at a time,
Before the hatred in her builds and finds herself staring at the bottom of a bottle.

A year prior, I'd started attending Al-Anon meetings, for family members of alcoholics, and so I headed to a meeting.

"The soundtrack to our Christmases always seems to be this old country song, 'Please Daddy Don't Get Drunk This Christmas,'" I told the support group.

"Ha! Of course there's a country song about a father who drinks too much and a daughter who wants to clean up a mess she didn't make."

The quip soothed my broken heart as I mourned the loss of the father I'd known and loved so fiercely as a child.

The Dada of my childhood was incredible: mischievous and fun and spontaneous. I waited longingly for him to return home from seemingly-interminable stretches of time away, mostly because life at home was sweeter when he was around.

One day, Achie was attempting to wake me from my afternoon nap. I was having none of it. Determined to cling to my naptime just a little bit longer, I heard Dada walk into the house. He'd been at the Casbah, drinking with his buddies for the afternoon, as was his habit when he was home.

"She's not getting up," complained Achie.

"Oh, I guess she doesn't want to go to the movies. I got tickets to her favourite show, and it starts soon!"

"Let's go!" I was suddenly wide awake and ready to rock.

I'd never been to the movies before. It was a Saturday afternoon, and my mother was at work. Dada had gotten tickets to my favourite action hero, He-Man, who had come to the big screen in *Masters of the Universe*. I loved sitting between him and Achie at the Bandra Talkies, as the lights dimmed. I was enthralled by the majesty of the big screen, the terror of Skeletor, and the power of Dolph Lundgren's He-Man! It was the best day ever.

That was my dad. Larger than life at 6'2", swooping in with joy, leaving an olfactory wake that was a combination of Marlboro cigarettes, Yardley's hair brilliantine, and Brut aftershave.

Dad was always an impermanent part of my life. He worked on oil rigs, mostly in the Persian Gulf when I was young, and did hitches of five weeks, which meant that he'd be gone for five weeks, often with very little contact, and then be home for five weeks. As a young child, I lived for his weeks at home.

Things at home were better when he was around. I didn't get beaten or screamed at. He came with toys and chocolate from his travels, and we got to do fun outings as a family. Dad was a social butterfly. My childhood home was always filled with his friends. Dad would meet up with them for motorcycle rides, eating, drinking, and merriment. When dad was home, my parents would throw lovely parties where all the grown-ups would dress in party frocks and dance the evening away. I loved dancing with the grown-ups. My dad was the best dance partner. He taught me to jive and foxtrot. My mum couldn't or wouldn't dance, and I was only too happy to be twirled around the dance floor at community parties, weddings, and the like. My dad had a deep, wonderful singing voice as well, and I loved hearing him strum his guitar, singing "*Solamente una vez.*"

From my dad, I inherited my love of old country music. Willie Nelson, Merle Haggard, Johnny Cash, Dolly Parton, George Jones. The list of legends is long, and my love for them is just as profound. When Dada was home, 4 o'clock was music time. He would awake from his afternoon nap and turn on our stereo, and we'd sing "Always on My Mind." When I was sad, I'd listen to Willie's lyrics, and imagine that that was what my Dada was singing to me when he was away: that even if he couldn't be there all the time, I was always on his mind.

I think my dad fancied himself a cowboy. With his Levi's jeans and large belt buckles, I believed that he was.

As a small child, it didn't matter that dad missed all the important days in my calendar. My needs were puny compared to what he was doing for the family. He worked hard and sacrificed so much so that I could have pretty dresses, fun toys, live in a nice house, take elocution classes, and go on holidays. All of this was true. My life growing up was infused with a healthy dose of financial privilege thanks to my father's work, which afforded us the opportunity to "earn in American dollars and live in Indian rupees," as my mother often said. I didn't fully comprehend what any of that meant. I just knew that when he was home, things were good.

Every weekend when dad was home, we'd wake up early and go to the Ramada Hotel at Juhu Beach. Dad had a friend on staff there, and we'd swim in the hotel pool for hours. I was amazed to watch dad stretch out his albatross-like wingspan, and then slice into the water off the high diving board. After hours in the pool, we'd eat hotel french fries, thick cut, salty goodness, doused in ketchup. A few years later, as a pre-teen, I would take up competitive swimming, hoping that dad would know that it was because the smell of chlorine and sunshine brought back the memories of that Ramada pool, where I felt buoyed by the blue water and the joy of hanging out with him.

Dad was also an exceptional storyteller, and I was enthralled by his fantastic tales. One day, deeply agitated, I rushed home from church:

"Dada! Dada!"

"What, *boochee?*"

"Father Nerus stole your story. He told your story in church today. How did he know it, Dada? Did you tell him?"

"What story, baby?"

"You know, the one you told me–about David and Goliath."

Dad's version of "David and Goliath" was the only one I'd ever known, and I was fuming with proprietary indignation that it had been blatantly plagiarized by the parish priest.

My favourite story of my father's was about Lionel, which he usually entertained me with while feeding me lunch on his days home. The story of Lionel was thrilling, and I demanded to hear it often. I particularly loved the parts of the story where Lionel's dad swoops in on a helicopter to battle a great crocodile. As far as I knew, this story was a creation of my dad's own imagination, but as with David and Goliath, who's to say for sure?

The story of Lionel epitomized the awe and wonder I felt for my dad. I imagined that if things got really bad in my life, or if I got into big trouble, my father would butcher a whole crocodile to save me. I worked hard to show him that I would be just as loyal in return.

In the evenings, when he'd sit down with a whiskey and some snacks, I'd offer to cut up cheese and ham for him to graze on. I'd cut the cheese a little thicker than necessary, just to show that he was my favourite. When he was done with his drink, I'd offer to pour him another one.

"Two fingers," he'd say, handing me his glass.

I learned quickly that he meant the width of *his* two fingers, not my much smaller ones. I'd top the whiskey up with water like he enjoyed, and learned through trial and error what shade of amber was too light for his liking because it meant I'd watered it down too much.

"Enough now, huh?" my mother would comment every so often as I returned with the glass of whiskey, raising her eyebrows at my dad, implying that he'd had enough and that I should stop pouring for him.

"It's OK Mama, I added lots of water," I'd assuage her.

At five, six, seven, eight years old, I had learned to broker peace and keep the two parties happy, one with whiskey, the other with water.

✻

My father became two drastically different people when he drank. In my younger days, Charlie emerged often. Charlie was who my dad would become if he were drunk and happy. Charlie was jovial, told jokes and stories, and laughed abundantly.

"How's dad doing?" I'd enquire on phone calls with my mother, long after I'd left their home.

"He's Charlie today."

I knew she meant that he was drunk but still happy.

When dad drank past Charlie, a second personality emerged, and it was never wise to stop and give a name to this iteration of my father. When this version of him showed up, it was wisest to shut up, scurry away, and keep things as peaceful and copacetic as possible.

My father at this stage of drunkenness was cruel, melancholic, sarcastic, and resentful. When this happened, Achie squirreled me off to bed. Sometimes I'd hear mum and dad arguing in the living room, or taking the row to their bedroom if it got too loud.

Achie would tuck me in with songs.

"Come baby. Let's go to bed. *Bésame, bésame mucho. Como si fuera, esta noche, la última vez.*"

"No, Achie. Sing 'Country Roads.'"

"Ok baby. Come. Sleep. Country roads, take me home. To the place, I belong…"

If Achie wasn't around, I'd put headphones over my ears, and allow whatever tape I was listening to to lull me to sleep. This auditory safety blanket of my childhood remains with me to this day.

✳

That second personality that emerged after Charlie is who my father has morphed into permanently now. It is him I've encountered each of the half-dozen times I've seen my father over the last decade. With this email that he's sent me, I fear I've lost every single thing that is precious to me from my childhood and adolescent years, including the jovial, tender man I knew to be my dad.

I now hold ferociously onto the precious gifts my father gave me before he became subsumed by that cruel, resentful, vitriolic part of himself. A solar-powered watch he gave me for my 15th birthday, a Swiss army knife that he won as a safety award, the mug he bought me at my undergrad convocation ceremony, which I was so proud he could attend. I have his big brown eyes and rosy cheeks. I have his hands, his hair, his love of good laughter. I have his penchant for melancholia, his drive, his generosity, and if I'm not careful with my own words, I know that they too can cut like a knife. I make sure to be careful.

For so long, in childhood, I waited for my Dada to

show up and save me.

"Things will be better when Dada is home," I would soothe myself.

I know now that while he wasn't able to rescue me, I can't save him either, and that part haunts a much younger part of me. If I were a better daughter, surely he'd have chosen me over his demons? For now, through my heartbreak, I cling tightly to my vision of the dad I used to know: tall and strong like those old cowboys he loved so much, like Lionel's croc-slaying father, like David who took down Goliath.

Feb 21, 2006

Growing up, I thought every dad drank every night..that every family dealt with it. it was no big deal. Now that I'm all grown up (or something like that), I'm finding it a challenge to believe that it's not my fault when he pours that whiskey.

Rationally, I know that I can't do a damn thing to control what he does to himself..what I seem to resent is what he's doing to me..to us. I used to think that if he loved us, he'd stop..I don't think that that's the reason he drinks though. I can't help but think that I'm not doing something I should be doing..being something better than I'm being..I can't help but feel guilty for talking too loudly and disrupting his whiskey-induced sleep, or saying something that may trigger a binge. Do I have to live in an eternal state of pussy-footing around my life? It's making me angry and bitter and that's one thing I don't want to see happen to me...I just wish I knew how to make it stop.

Viva la Revolución

Still feeling sucker-punched from my father's email, I am now wondering how to share this pain with my partner, Dustin. I feel sick at the prospect of betraying my father's alcoholism to someone outside the family. It is drilled deep into my being that I am never to reveal family secrets. Save for a very few exceptions, for which I have always felt immense guilt, I have adhered to this rule.

Dustin and I have been together only six short months. In that time, I have spent a significant amount of time away from him, traveling for my doctoral research. A few weeks earlier, while on a research trip, I had invited him to visit me and meet my parents. My father had been drunk and my mother had been standoffish. I felt ashamed to have taken my new partner, whom I was so enthralled with, into such a noxious environment. I worried he would consider them a reflection of my worth, my badness, and so choose to distance himself from me.

In the time that Dustin and I have been dating, I've come to realize that allowing myself to be loved is a revolutionary act.

When we first met, something in me recognized something in him. This recognition of myself in another felt overwhelming, compelling, scary even. Perhaps we were once made of the same star. Maybe something in his eyes reminded me of myself. It might have been that his intensity matched my own, and I felt seen. I felt a compulsion to message him. So I did.

Our first date, in the dead of a Calgary winter, was meant to last one beer. It lasted ten hours. Over drinks, we got into a vocabulary-based debate, about the meaning of a particular word.

"What are the stakes? What do I get if I win?" I am forever competitive.

"Hmmm. What if, loser makes dinner for our next date? Winner brings the wine," he suggested.

"Deal!" I was convinced I'd win. I did not.

Though I didn't love that I had lost, I liked that he was neither afraid to challenge me, nor daunted by my competitiveness.

A few days later, he invited me over to his place for wine and music.

"What the hell does 'wine and music' mean? Is it code for something?" I fretted over the phone with a friend.

I changed my outfit a few times. Dustin picked me up and drove us to his home. We sipped wine and, an audiophile, he took me through his musical loves, and we talked into the wee hours of the morning. Then, only a few hours before he had to be at work, he drove me back to my place. Wine and music, it turned out, was just that. I have come to learn that Dustin doesn't speak in codes.

I made good on my promise to cook him dinner. I made a homemade pasta dish: spicy Italian sausage and spinach in a cream sauce. The wine bottle that he brought to keep his end of the deal now sits, months later and empty, on the kitchen counter in my apartment.

"You know you sing when you enter your kitchen? And your whole body changes."

Nobody had ever seen me in that way before, deeper than just the surface. We talked for hours that night, and he stayed over. The next morning, knowing my love of greasy spoon diners, he took me to the diviest spot, the Deerhead Cafe. In those first days, I was a walking mass of anxiety, worried that at any moment he would realize that I was entirely too much to handle. My jokes would be too off colour, my goals too ambitious, my questions too challenging.

*

"If she doesn't *sudrao*, she'll have a tough time finding a man to put up with her."

It was the summer before Dustin and I met, and my mother hadn't known that I was within earshot of her comment. I was always being told to *sudrao*, improve. Be less dramatic, less gregarious, less me. Just…less.

This demand to be less than my full self has been a constant refrain for as long as I've been me: questioning, challenging, curious, expansive me.

An early instance of this found me putting my questioning mind up against a bastion of my childhood: the Catholic church.

It was the middle of the night before my First Confession, and the glow of the television illuminated my insomnia. I was anxious about having to tell Fr. Nereus about all the sins that I had committed. I seemed to sin a lot, or so I'd been told. Fr. Nereus had known me since infancy. In fact, he'd known my father since infancy, and he was now our parish priest. He'd baptized both me and my brother in the same ancient church that generations of my family had been baptized in. Fr. Nereus was always giving out candy after Mass. He seemed ethereal, calm and passionate all at the same time. I loved him with a healthy mix of admiration, awe, and fear. I'd heard tales of his strictness from dad, who had had Fr. Nereus as a schoolmaster at St. Andrews many years before.

What would I tell Fr. Nereus the next day, I wondered.

"Forgive me, Father, for I have sinned. Today is my first confession."

I practiced the script that I'd been taught in catechism class.

> *My God, I am sorry for my sins with all*
> *my heart.*
> *In choosing to do wrong and failing to do*
> *good, I have sinned against You whom I*
> *should love above all things.*
> *I firmly intend, with Your help, to do*
> *penance, to sin no more, and to avoid*
> *whatever leads me to sin.*
> *Our Saviour Jesus Christ suffered and*
> *died for me.*
> *In his name, Lord please have mercy.*

In the darkened living room, I whispered this prayer, the *Act of Contrition*, that I would need to say in the confessional booth the next day. The only witnesses to my insomniac rehearsal were a bevy of men in tight white *chuddies*, gyrating on the Phil Donohue show. I had the TV volume turned down so I wouldn't disturb anyone in the house, but the dancing men and Phil were able to provide sufficient distraction from my deep dark secret. I had sinned big time!

You see, in catechism class, Aunty Maureen had taught us all about the sacrament of Holy Communion, and how our catechism was to prepare us to be spiritually and physically purified to receive the body of Christ at the sacrament of our First Holy Communion. Dad had bought me a pair of bright white shoes on his last trip, and Mama had taken me to the tailor aunty to get my pristine white communion dress sewn. The big day, December 8, was arriving soon, and I was so excited because for once, dad would be home for one of my big days! The last big hurdle after having gone through a year of catechism classes was for me to make my First Confession, which would purify me of my sins before receiving Christ into my heart.

One day, in catechism class, I asked, "Aunty Maureen, why can't I receive communion with everyone else?"

"No, my girl. That is not allowed. First you must make your First Confession, and only then are you purified to receive the Body of Christ."

This unsatisfactory response begged further investigation on my part.

I usually attended the 8 am children's Mass at St. Andrews. I loved singing in the choir with my friends and getting candy from Fr. Nereus afterwards. Plus, my parents went to the later service so I was *bindaas* to do and be as I pleased. Sometimes Achie came with me, and sometimes I went alone, walking the ten minutes from our flat to the church with all my neighbourhood friends.

One Sunday, after my question to Aunty Maureen, when all the adults were queuing up to receive communion, I decided to join them. I wanted to know what was so special about this forbidden sacrament thing. As I made my way up to the front of the church, I eyed everyone around me guiltily. Surely someone would stop me or know that I hadn't yet received my First Holy Communion, and was thus ineligible to be in this line. My unpurified heart and I edged closer and closer to the priest handing out the wafers.

"Body of Christ."

"Amen."

"Body of Christ."

"Amen."

"Body of Christ."

"Amen."

Ok, you have to say 'Amen' before taking the communion, I coached myself.

Mimicking the adults around me, I was duly solemn. Soon, I was at the front of the line.

"Body of Christ," said the priest, motioning to place the wafer on my tongue.

"Amen!!!"

I had done it. I had eaten the body of Christ himself. Nice crunch, weird aftertaste.

I made my way back to the pew, kneeling with feigned gravitas to fit in. No one had noticed. Nothing bad happened. Nothing inside me felt different. Weird.

I replicated my experiment again the following week, and once more the week after that. Three weeks in and still I felt no change, spiritual, emotional, nothing! I wondered if maybe the magic didn't work without the sacrament?

Someone from the neighbourhood finally saw me and informed Aunty Maureen that one of her catechists had gone rogue. I had to do a special drawing in my catechism notebook, and I would have to tell Fr. Nereus about it at my First Holy Confession.

This was the grave sin that wouldn't let me sleep. My soul's eternal salvation was at stake. I wondered if Phil Donohue or the dancing *chuddi*-clad men went to confession. What did they reveal to their parish priests?

The following day, Fr. Nereus gave me ten Hail Marys and a few Our Fathers as penance. It seemed a small price to pay to safeguard my eternal salvation while also testing my hypothesis.

✳

Not all my childhood rebellions ended up quite as well. It wasn't long after I confessed my sins to Fr. Nereus that I found myself sitting with my father, across from a child psychologist.

"Ok, what does that mean?" My dad was confused. "Her mother and I have tried everything we can think of. She just won't behave. My wife is ready to give up on her."

I felt as though the chair under me was about to give way. How could Dad tell the doctor that I was so bad that Mom wanted to give me away? I sang a song in my head so that Dad and the doctor wouldn't know. The song, which I'd recently learned at school, was about an orphan nobody wanted because she was blind.

Ever since I'd learned the song, I had been singing it to myself when I felt sad or lonely or scared, or at bedtime. I imagined what it might be like to be a blind orphan and have nobody want me. Some days it didn't feel like my life was that different from that orphan's. Some days I kind of wished it were true.

It was confusing to have Dad with me at the appointment. He was rarely at any of my events, and if he did come, it was definitely only *with* Mom. That morning had been bad at home though.

"I'm fed up with you," my mother had screamed at me. "I wish I'd stayed in the convent and never gotten married or been cursed with you."

Then she turned her rage on my father: "You take her. I'm always running after her. I'm fed up. She's your daughter. I don't want to have anything to do with her."

I spent the whole trip to the doctor's trying to cheer Dad up because I knew it was my fault my parents had fought, and I didn't want him to hate me as well.

The doctor who was talking to Dad was nothing like Dr. Hebbar, our family doctor. I had met this doctor a few weeks ago in a big white classroom where she gave me puzzles and sheets of maths problems to solve. Then she gave Mama a booklet of puzzles I needed to do at home and bring back with me to this appointment. The doctor pulled up all my tests.

"She placed in the 85th percentile of IQ for her age group," the doctor said. "She's incredibly intelligent. Where does she go to school? How is she doing there?"

"Umm…my wife, her mother, usually brings Roselle to these kinds of things."

My father was flustered. It was unnerving. He didn't answer the doctor's questions.

"They've been getting into fights, and my wife can't handle her anymore."

I wondered if maybe he was still angry with me for making Mom angry with him.

When we got home, he dropped the papers that the doctor had given him, on the dining table. My mother was in bed, the door firmly shut.

Dad poured a drink. I knew afternoon drinking meant evening fighting and I tried to mitigate that inevitability by making up with my mother on my father's behalf.

"Mama. Mama," I knocked at her bedroom door. "The doctor said I scored really high on that test. She said I'm smart! Come on, Mama," I pleaded.

"I'm coming. Give me some time."

Phew! I grinned at dad as I raced past the hall, where he sat and tended to his whiskey. Phew.

✹

A few weeks prior to visiting the IQ doctor, my mother had taken me to a different doctor's appointment.

We didn't usually go to Holy Family Hospital, but my mother said that we needed to go see a doctor there because my school teacher had told us to go. My mother seemed nervous, and it was already dark outside. Usually

Dr. Hebbar came home if it was after dark, but Mama said this was the only time the doctor could see us, and that he was a different kind of doctor than Dr. Hebbar.

"Dr. Hebbar is for when you have *boo boos* on your body. This doctor is going to try and help us with your misbehaviour. Remember to show him how good you can be."

I was keen to follow my mother's coaching, hoping against hope that my badness wouldn't emerge.

I was fidgety as we waited for the doctor. I watched the scurrying nurses in their crisp white outfits and smart box hats. Watching them helped me imagine what they were doing: tending to patients, giving needles, taking blood pressures. Thinking about the details of their jobs helped me feel less squiggly in my seat.

This doctor's office was not like Dr. Hebbar's at all. This doctor didn't give me candy or use a stethoscope on my heart and let me listen. This office was full of papers and books, and the fan was making everything blowy.

I sat in the corner seat at his wooden desk, and Mama sat beside me. They talked about my problems. My school had told Mama to bring me here because I'd failed a big exam and they were saying maybe I needed to be in a special school.

"She's not backwards or anything," my mother assured the doctor. "She knows all the answers, she just doesn't like to write them down. Or sit still. Her teachers are always complaining that she's distracting everyone around her, but she knows all the answers. Two years ago, when my son was born, we threw her a big birthday party, and she invited the whole class, without telling us. She just acts carelessly. She doesn't think."

In my defense, though my parents had extended invitations to my sixth birthday party to a few of my neighbourhood and school friends, I was compelled to invite the other kids in my classroom to the party because they were sad at not having been invited. I couldn't bear to leave them out. It was an excellent and boisterous birthday party, and I regret nothing.

I couldn't believe my mother was telling the doctor all these bad things I had done. She had told me to show him how good I was, and now he would know that I wasn't good.

Once my mother and the doctor finished discussing me and my behaviour, as if I weren't even in the room, the doctor turned to me and began asking me questions. His questions were boring, and he kept writing things down. He didn't look at me or talk to me like Dr. Hebbar did.

After all his questions were over, the doctor sat back with the end of his pen in his mouth.

"You're right," he told my mother. "She's not backwards, but she might be bored in school. Have you gotten her IQ tested? I know a great child psychologist in town who would do the testing. I can send you to her."

My mother took the papers he gave her, and we left. Though I didn't like that doctor very much, I felt good leaving Holy Family Hospital. He was the first adult who didn't think I was bad or broken, and something about how he said I was smart made me feel calm.

✷

Things at home had been decidedly *not* calm for a while. Ever since I had failed that big exam that had landed me in those doctors' offices.

Teacher Amy had helped us prepare all year long for the upcoming 3rd Standard Maharashtra state exam, a standardized test to ensure that pupils were maintaining academic standards at the primary level before entering the middle school years.

Days after I had taken the test, I was handed back a failed result. I had scored a big fat goose egg. Zero points on the test meant that I had to take a note home to my mother, which requested her presence at a meeting with Teacher Amy and the principal.

On the test, I had written my name and had left the rest of it blank. I knew that giving my mother the note would not be good. I was not wrong.

"They're going to think I didn't teach you anything!" my mother screamed at me as she took a *chappal* off her foot to hit me. The failing grade seemed to offer a perjurious reflection of the hours that my mother and her cane had poured into helping me study for that exam.

A few days later, in the principal's office, with Teacher Amy present, a far gentler version of my mother presented itself.

"Why, Roselle?" she enquired tenderly. "We studied together. You know all the answers to these questions."

My mother's tone was a signal for me to not embarrass her in front of the school administrators, and in an effort to demonstrate to them that she had in fact done her duty as a responsible parent, she began quizzing me, demanding impromptu answers to the questions on the test sheet.

"See? She knows the answers," she crowed triumphantly to the other adults in the room, when I answered the on-the-spot quiz successfully. She had fulfilled her duty as a caring mother, and my failure was now mine alone to bear.

She turned back to me, now that her name had been cleared, and repeated her query: "If you know all the answers, why didn't you write it down?"

I looked at my mother. I looked at Teacher Amy. I looked at the stern-faced nun who was principal at the time.

"I know the answers. Teacher Amy knows the answers. Why do I have to write them down?"

✹

Landing in trouble from asking problematic questions would fill me with shame for a long time.

Many years later, this shame would rear its villainous head when I was fired from my first professional role after grad school. Fresh out of my doctorate and wanting to change the world, I would embark on a career in the field of diversity & inclusion, a professional landscape in its absolute nascence at the time. I would find myself working at a non-profit organization, where I did frontline work with clients, facilitated community conversations, while also leading a team. I would be a top performer at the organization for two years in a row, with glowing client reviews, and community organizations seeking me out by name to facilitate their learnings, and a thriving team.

Alas, none of this would be sufficient to save me from the ax that swung when I dared ask some pesky questions.

My boss frequently screamed at many of us, often making ego-driven decisions on a whim. Once, when I observed that none of our client services was particularly tailored for the large Indigenous client group that we served, and suggested the possibility of the organization's service providers undertaking culturally-appropriate training, she sneered at me: "You're lucky you're the right kind of Indian, or you wouldn't even be here."

When my boss accused me of being too challenging, too difficult, not respectful enough, it was like being, once again, on the receiving end of my mother's screams. I tried to placate and pacify, to turn down the heat that would inevitably burn me. My boss's barbed words flew at me: *challenging, difficult, disloyal, ungrateful.* Words that would find resounding echoes in the way my parents saw me, and would slice at the same wounds and scar tissue.

Just as in my childhood, being screamed at by my boss would throw me into my survival response: an instinctive reaction to keep myself as pleasing as possible and exit the situation as quickly as I could.

Over my lifetime, I have learned that my two main responses under attack are to flee and to fawn: I want to run away, and barring that as a possibility, I want to smile and make things as copacetic as possible, so the aggressor will no longer see me as a threat, leaving me free to skedaddle to safety.

I know now that this is something that many women and folks from marginalized genders do to keep safe in dangerous situations, where fighting and fleeing are not viable options.

I would try in vain to assuage my boss, wondering what I had done to elicit such vitriolic behaviour. Being berated, willing myself not to cry, and simultaneously remembering the shame of being a bad child.

After months of experiencing and observing horrifying treatment at this job, I finally asked for answers. Why was I paid less than my peers? Why was a portion of my salary withheld without notice for months following a promotion? As I asked for clarity, wave after wave of fear crashed through me.

The day after my questions, I was unceremoniously released from my job, escorted out like a criminal, all of my office tchotchkes in a cardboard box, like a seen-on-

TV cliché.

"I think I need to apply for EI," I lamented to Dustin soon after being let go. "But I don't want to."

"What's stopping you?"

"I don't want to apply to EI because now I'm the stereotype of what anti-immigrant sentiments spew: an immigrant, coming here, and living off the system. I don't want to be that person."

"You've worked and paid into the system since you were 15 years old. You are allowed to lean into that support when you need to, now."

None of the reasonable and logical points that Dustin offered assuaged my shame, and this experience would drown me in months of depression.

Asking questions of big systems has been part of the fabric of being me for so long, and the penalties for asking those questions, particularly as a racialized immigrant woman invested in the work of dismantling systemic oppression, are high. The systems are designed to put people who dare ask such questions in our place.

Jan 4

I feel under water today. Every time I sit down I get stuck and cannot move or get up.

I did not act in a way that was immoral or unethical. I asked some questions and pointed out incongruencies. I spoke truth to power. Sadly, there seem to be ramifications for that.

I did good work with integrity and good ethics. I can and will be proud of that.

After nearly a year of bullying and constant harassment, racial tokenization, and abuse, I finally named the pattern of behaviour and requested a mediated conversation. Instead, today, I was pulled into the CEOs office and at 4:46PM, I was let go, being told that I was "not a fit" for the organization. Let go without cause, and with a handsome payout so I wouldn't seek legal action.

How could I have been fired? ne'er-do-wells are fired. Losers are fired. People who are not good at their jobs, who are lazy, who cheat and lie....those people get fired. If the moral arc of the universe bends towards justice-and a part of me continues to believe that it does-then how could I have been fired for doing nothing wrong?

I feel hurt and heartbroken and grieved about this absolute failure.

✴

Prickly shame courses through my body now, as I contemplate the very thought of sharing my father's email with Dustin.

This email, with all its jabs and barbs, has been ostensibly provoked by me having dared to share my new mailing address with my parents, because Dustin and I have moved in together. How can my choice to live with someone whom I adore be a bad thing? I'm 28 years old, and haven't lived with them for a decade. How is this any of their damn business? Is *this* cause enough to disown me as their daughter? My mind is tumultuous and vacillating between reasoning my way through these questions, and being sucked into the roiling waters of my emotions. I feel like I'm drowning, and I cannot simply think my way out of it.

The email from my father is peppered with words that pierce at my deepest fears of myself:

Fatted...ungrateful...greedy...disrespectful...your pride will come before a great fall...

The words in my father's email are not qualities I see in myself, but if someone who's known me my entire life has seen me this way for so long, is there some truth to these assessments of my character? If being myself has provoked these assessments from people around me, then maybe I *am* these things? I am terrified that sharing this email with Dustin will make him worry that there might be truth to these barbed words.

Unable to catch my breath, or hear anything past the rushing in my ears, I recall the first time that Dustin told me I am easy to love. Not *that* he loves me, or that I am lovable. But that I am *easy* to love. That all my warts and too much-ness are not barriers to the ease with which he loves me. When I first heard him, primed to believe that I am chronically unloveable, I felt nauseated. Remembering his words now, makes me feel calm. It will be years before I dare to fully believe him. In the darkest recesses of my slithering fears, albeit with increasingly less frequency, I will continue to doubt it for a long time.

Grief, Rage, Compassion

"Roselle, he's just drunk. Ignore it."

I am talking out loud to myself in the empty apartment, hoping that keeping my voice calm will settle the rising bile. Zeke, our dog, piques his head at me. I guess the apartment isn't empty after all. The little four-legged angel looks at me curiously. I am speaking in the same tone I use on him when he is feeling cranky. He cocks his head, as if to say, "I'm not cranky, why are you calming me down?"

Zeke pops the illusory bubble of calm in which this horrifying email is no big deal. I gulp big dollops of air that suddenly seem too thick. My hands begin to shake, and the room gets darker. Maybe if I open the curtains I'll be able to breathe? It is a bit after 7:30 am and Dustin has just left for work. I have a day of paper writing ahead of me. I also need to prepare for my upcoming research trip to India. I am slated to leave in ten days.

"I don't have time for this," I say to Zeke.

I can't stop staring at the email. I pick up the twelve-pound doxie around whom my world revolves.

"I guess we can sit, but just for a minute."

I sit on the couch, and place him on my chest. His body presses on my sternum and air rushes from my ineffectual lungs. I am a deflating balloon. Empty, nothingness envelops me.

"No, Roselle," I admonish out loud. "You cannot let this get to you. You have a paper to write, and you have to prepare for tomorrow's class."

Zeke has fallen asleep my chest as if none of this really matters. My love for him makes my heart swell in a way that envelops the rage roiling within me. The shock of the email is morphing into red hot anger. Over many years of therapy, I have become familiar with my anger. While I am not angry by nature, rage has coursed through me for as long as I can remember.

I used to hate going to *Kottase* Papa and Nana's house as a small child. They lived just one street over, and they were always drunk. To this day, the smell of old urine takes me right back to their ground floor flat, the scents of pomelo trees and the Arabian Sea breeze doing nothing to disguise the stench. *Kottase* Papa and Nana were dad's parents. My mother had told me to call them this to differentiate them from her father, my Papa, who lived with us. *Kottase*, a particularly cruel adjective in hindsight for a child to be armed with, means "liquor" in Marathi. It was a nod to their alcoholism, which my mother equated with their lack of class and character. Visiting them after

5 pm was always a bad idea. The booze would have been flowing for long enough that belligerence, yelling, and often fisticuffs were inevitable. I never wanted to visit, and was never allowed not to.

In my four-year-old wisdom, as soon as their tones got heated, making me feel scared and angry, I would ask for a glass of water. I'd sip a bit, and then with all the rage in my heart, I'd bite down hard. The glass shattered in my mouth, and my parents would take us home. Mission accomplished.

I bit through four glasses before the adults got wise to my antics and started using a stainless steel cup for my water. I learned that actions I took when enraged could help to get me out of situations in which I felt scared and unsafe. My rage was also a telltale indicator that my core sense of justice was being challenged.

Shortly after Teacher Francesca became our class teacher in the first standard, she decreed that the mini blackboard beside her big one would be a reward for well-behaved students and special occasions. This junior chalkboard came complete with plenty of chalk and a sturdy wooden chalk duster. At lunchtime, the child who'd been really good or the child whose birthday it was, was given permission to use it for as long as they liked. Since I was never particularly good at sitting still or not talking to my friends in class, I stood a zero percent chance of achieving lunchtime dominion over the mini board. I knew for certain though, that on my birthday, the board would be mine, and I was ready! I'd made plans for what I'd draw.

My birthday finally arrived. And, so did a new kid. At lunchtime, before any of us were done having our lunch, she strutted her patent leather Mary Janes over to the mini board and started drawing on it. Aghast at the audacity, I rushed over to explain the rule about birthdays and being good and how it was finally my one time to use the coveted mini board. She bore me no mind and said something about an early bird.

Fists clenched, I huffed over to where Teacher Francesca sat. I *had* tried to reason with the new girl, after all.

"Teacher, teacher. She won't give me my board. I told her it's my birthday, even."

"It's ok, it's ok. She doesn't know, nah? Just let her use it for now, she's already there, no? You take it after, or even tomorrow, maybe."

Teacher's soothing was useless. I stomped back to my seat, eyeing my nemesis. Out of the corner of my eye, I spied the chalk duster, a solid block of wood with a side of green felt. Righteous anger filling my veins, I picked it up and threw it at her head. My aim has always been true.

Blood spilled from the cut in the new girl's forehead, tears from her eyes, and I never got a chance at the damn mini board ever again.

All my rage is present now, as Zeke snores gently on my chest. I watch his body rise and fall with my sobbing. He carries on sleeping. Zeke is one of the very best beings to have ever blessed me with his love.

Dustin got Zeke from a friend whose toddler mistook the dachshund for a horse and kept trying to ride him. Zeke didn't take too kindly to this indignity, and nipped at the child, which prompted the adult to rehome the dog. Zeke suffered no fools—one of many traits he and I shared. A year after Zeke and Dustin joined forces,

I came into their lives. Our pack of three was neurotic, stubborn, loyal, loving.

Zeke is my first pet, and the first being outside of myself whom I've had to be responsible for. He has taught me more about myself than I could imagine.

Loving Zeke continues to open mirrors onto myself; to *all* parts of myself. Loving him reveals my amazing and ugly bits. I love nurturing him, feeding him, cuddling him. And I really love that he loves me back. On the flip side, I have learned that I hate being needed, or being beholden. My loss of independence is something I resist ferociously. Making room for Zeke's needs and my emotions reminds me that I owe him the best in me. I deeply cherish his trust in me, and I count on his cheekiness. His love is the very thing that has offered me healing.

Through Zeke, I learn the true meaning of compassion, even in the face of rage and heartbreak.

It has always been difficult to know that I wasn't the child my parents wanted. While they definitely wanted a child, they were ill-equipped to handle what I, in particular, presented. I was questioning, challenging, boisterous, energetic, difficult to control, and not particularly fond of being told what to do. I was difficult to love. I know this because they repeatedly told me so.

My father's sense of parental duty, which had been elusive most of my life, came into sharp focus after he retired from his travel-heavy career. By then, I was well into my 20s, and hadn't needed hands-on parenting for some time. I think he felt rejected that I'd grown up while he'd been away. He wanted to be needed as a child would need him; I'd learned not to need him and was no longer a child.

My mother resented me, first for having cost her those precious last moments with her own mother. Then, to add insult to injury, I was the firstborn in a family of plenty, showered with so many resources right from the start. She had grown up, the middle child of middle children, with barely any access to food and education, nevermind resources or attention. I had been handed the life she so desperately longed for.

Staring at Zeke on my chest, my emotions collide.

As the weight of my father's email sets in, the grief and rage of it all feel too enormous to hold. Injustice, unfairness, unsafety all seem to trigger my rage. I know that my anger protects me from all that I cannot control, all that makes me feel powerless and small. For that, I am eternally grateful. Over the years, I've learned to listen to my anger when she growls, so that she doesn't have to roar–or hurl chalk dusters at peoples' heads. Now, my anger emerges only on rare occasions, often accompanied by her comrade, compassion.

Processing the chaos of emotions surging through my body leaves me catatonic on the couch. Time is meaningless, and seven hours float by as I oscillate between sobs and rage. Zeke stays on my chest through it all. Every so often, he sighs, as if comprehending the weight of the world that I've lost today.

For now, we sit together on the couch of my darkened apartment, me a ball of exposed nerve endings, and him, a snoring darling, calmly soothing my distraught nervous system.

As I think about my relationship with my parents, I feel grief over my roots. That is a big deal - connection to culture and family past. That is a huge deal - I looong for those roots to be cultivated. I think that's where the yearning to be in touch with my parents comes from...even though every shred of evidence I have has told me time and time again, every reconnection brings pain, heartbreak, manipulation, derision. But I yearn for it-even if it's just superficial. Just so I can say that I have parents...a girl with no parents is such a suspicious thing. I do not believe that my dream for a healing together with them will ever manifest itself in this life. And it's not actually pertinent to my own healing and growth whether it does or not, I suppose. I may never get resolution. I grieve over the potential that will never be - we don't get to have that this time around. In this life, I can only hold compassion for how they came to be... and compassion for myself for what I cannot be... to and for them.

Loss is a Four Letter Word

"Babe," I text Dustin, "I'm OK, but…"

Isn't shock a wonderful thing? It allows me to calmly tell my beloved partner that I'm OK in a moment when I most certainly should not be calm. This is my way of not worrying him too much about exactly how OK I am (not).

"I got a pretty shocking email from my dad, and I don't know what to do about it."

"Another one?" Dustin's response is almost immediate.

Though we've only been dating six months, already he's been witness to a number of interactions with my father. A few months prior, after visiting my parents' home in Southern Ontario, he gently–so as not to overstep the fragility of a new romance–observed:

"I have never seen a parent talk to their child with

as much contempt and disgust as your parents talk to you. It's like they abhor you."

Having him validate what I've felt to be true for so many years was like having a light switched on, even though I didn't want to believe what was in front of me.

"If I send it to you, can you promise to only read it if you have the bandwidth for it?" I am trying to have as few needs as possible in our new romance, even as I feel my world caving in.

"I always have space for you."

Within minutes of sending him the email, he calls me.

"I'm coming home."

"No no. I have loads of stuff I need to do. Don't worry about me, I'm OK." That morsel of tasty nonsense again. If I can have as few needs as possible, I won't be too tedious to love. I don't want to inconvenience him.

"I wish I could come home and hold you, and we can talk about this. We can solve it together. What do you need? You can take time to think about it, but if you want to go back there and get anything from their house, we can go."

There are not enough neural pathways in my brain to process what he is saying. I am leaving for India in ten days. There's no way I can get to Ontario and back before then. Besides, I am flat broke, and neither one of us is in a position to spend money on a throwaway trip.

Dustin comes home early. I haven't yet gotten off the couch, and Zeke is still firmly in place on my chest. Dustin wraps himself around us.

"What do you need?" he asks tenderly, wiping the fat tears that won't stop rolling down my cheeks.

"I don't know. I haven't eaten. Zeke needs to go

outside."

On our walk around the neighbourhood, the sunlight feels like an affront. My world has been tilted off its axis. How dare the sun shine so flagrantly? Afterwards, we find ourselves back on the couch.

Dustin gently presses again: "Your things. What do you need from that house? You're gone for six months, and then it'll be too late to get them."

"There are some books and curios. My yearbooks, my photos, and journals from high school and university. My book of goodbyes from when I left India that has all my elementary school friends in it. My great-grandmother's ruby earring that I got on my 21st birthday. My WWF sticker collection."

Ten-year-old me collected those stickers with so much pride and joy, which only compounded as the collection grew over the years.

"Oh no. The bookshelf I built with my dad, and was saving to bring to our house. He said he sawed it in half and threw it away. All my precious things…they're…gone."

My tears reemerge at the weight of this loss.

"I never really looked at the sticker book," I try consoling myself. "Besides, someday I'll die, and none of this will matter. It doesn't matter."

Dustin remains silent. I think I am doing a good job of convincing him that none of those things matter.

"The only thing…" I stop.

Dustin looks at me.

"It's just…I can't…I'll never be able to replace it…"

Zeke has been a calming weight on my chest all day. Suddenly he feels like an anvil, and I hand him to Dustin. I sit up, struggling to breathe.

After twelve hours of everything being OK, the dam

bursts in body-wracking sobs.

"I didn't know how much it would mean to me five years ago when I tucked it into the bookshelf in my room at their house. I just left it there in an old plastic bag. It's the last thing I have left of my Papa."

Dustin stares at me as my sobs die down.

"My Papa's tile. It's gone."

Witness

It has been 48 hours since I received my father's email. I am struggling to get out of bed. Despite the last two nightmarish days, I have been able to hold it together enough so that nobody outside of Dustin and I knows about the despair swirling inside me.

I even taught my class yesterday. As I stepped into the room, I got a text from Lydia:

"Yo! What happened? I went over to your parent's house for something yesterday and there was lots of drama there."

Shaken, I didn't know how to reply to Lydia.

"I'm teaching a class in ten minutes," I texted. "Can't talk now. My dad wrote me an email. You know, the usual kind. He said I'm no longer their daughter and not welcome in their house anymore. And that all my stuff that's at their house is going in the garbage. I'll text you more later. I can't really process right now."

Grateful for the intellectual distraction, for 90 minutes I focused on delivering material that I felt confident about. Such a stark contrast from the crushing uncertainty of my personal life.

After class, Lydia's response was waiting:

"Oh man. Yea, that explains why they were screaming at each other. It kind of makes sense though that your dad would write that to you. You guys haven't been getting along a lot since you moved to Calgary…I think you really hurt them when you moved."

Lying in bed this morning, I play Lydia's text over and over in my mind.

Please be on my side, I want to beg her. *You're my best friend. My best friend.*

Asking her to be on my side was out of bounds for our friendship though.

Over the years, I shared snippets with Lydia about how bad things were between my parents and me. She loves them, and I didn't want to taint her love of them, or betray my parents. So I never shared the depths of my pain with her. And I suppose I didn't create much space for her to share her heart with me either.

We had been each other's go-to gal pal for nearly two decades, but in this rift with my parents, Lydia will choose them over me. After this text exchange, she will ghost me without reason, after a lifetime of friendship. Perhaps we had outgrown the garments of our youth. Where once we'd aimed our sharp tongues and eye rolls at the world around us, over time, we had turned them on each other. I had once thought of sarcasm as our love language, but I have come to understand that it is not actually a personality trait. Sarcasm is a linguistic sign of contempt.

I feel like a child, wanting to plead for someone to be on my side. But I can't fault her for loving my parents. They'd once described her as the daughter they wish they'd had.

✹

"Do you want me to stay home from work today?" Dustin pulls me out of my perseverations.

"No no," I assure him. "I have lots to do today. And I'm seeing the therapist later."

After Lydia's text message yesterday, I beelined to the university's Wellness Centre to book an appointment with a counselor. I knew I would need help unraveling this situation.

Now, I'm not so sure about that decision. Every counselor I've ever tried to open up to about my parents has asked me the same stupid thing: "Have you tried talking to them?"

"What should I tell her?" I ask Dustin as he's getting ready for work. "She's going to be the same as the others."

"What if you just tell her all of it? Don't sugarcoat it. Don't try to protect their reputation or minimize your experiences. They've abused you for years."

I don't like Dustin using that word. It seems as though he's attacking them, and if there's one thing my parents have ingrained in me, it's that you don't let outsiders talk poorly about your family. Always maintain the appearance of family unity, no matter what.

"They didn't abuse me," I clip back. "I'm making a big deal of this because I'm angry, but this is just their way."

"Why don't you like calling how they've treated you 'abuse'?" He is tender in his question.

Unnerved by the question and his calm, I turn away from him, and bury my face in his pillows. His scent calms me.

"Because…I don't want to be a victim," I muffle into the cotton pillowcase, now wet with tears. I hope he hasn't heard me.

"Just tell the counselor everything. You deserve to be heard. And you're not a victim. You've just been through a lot. I hope she can help you process some of it."

He strokes my back gently, kisses me on the head, and leaves for work.

This is the scene with which I open my session with the counselor. For the first time, I tell of the really ugly parts of my life—parts that I've never aired before, not even to myself.

As the end of our hour together approaches, I am eager to wrap the session in a neat bow of resolution and show the counselor how much I've learned in just one session. I shrug away the slimy entrails of my story, wiping snot with the last tissue in the box beside my chair.

"It's OK. I think I just need to recognize that they have a different way of being in the world than I do. They're from a different generation, and maybe it's part of the culture they were raised in. I'd like to recognize how to live with those differences."

Thick black horn-rimmed glasses and blood-red shoes, the counselor is tender and tentative in what she offers.

"Hmmm. Maybe. Maybe that's their culture, and I know exactly how difficult it is when we live between cultures. Maybe you *do* just need to recognize how to live with it."

This counselor is the first racialized therapist I've ever visited. She gets it, this sensation of being stuck between one world and another. I let her tentative response sink in. It doesn't seem like she's agreeing with me. Is she not buying my plan for wrapping up this session in a tidy lesson learned?

She continues: "Let's imagine you befriend a little girl. Sho tells you that she gets whipped every day at home, that she has to urinate on herself while her parents laugh, that she gets told over and over that her mother wishes she'd had an abortion instead of having her. What would you, the adult you, the wise you that is in front of me today…what would you say happened to that little girl?"

Having my own words and experiences repeated back to me by this outsider shakes me. Devoid of cultural context, filial piety, and the venomous vines that bind, the details are shocking. At this moment, I can't picture a world in which I am OK with someone else experiencing those shocking things.

"I would protect her," I say. "I'd call the police or child protective services."

"And what would you tell the police or child protective services?"

Lord, how I wish I had Dustin's pillow to sink my face into right now. There is nothing to muffle my words. Compelled by the counselor's invitation to bear witness to my own lived experiences, big fat tears roll slowly down my cheeks.

"I'd tell them the girl is being abused."

Family Chosen

"Ugh. I can't find a single place to rent for less than a year."

The week since receiving my father's email has been tumultuous. The research trip to India, which I've been planning for the better part of three years, is imminent. Prior to the email, I had accommodations for the months-long trip secured at my parent's flat in Bombay. The offer to stay there was rescinded in the email, and I now have less than two weeks to secure temporary housing in a country whose housing market I am completely unfamiliar with. Adrift on a sea of uncertainty, I feel scared and alone.

Scouring the online rental boards yields, at best, meager offerings, and at worst, scams that would be dangerous for a woman traveling alone. At the advice of a friend, I resort to social media. For all its many faults, not the least of which is the takedown of modern Western democracy, at this moment, Facebook becomes a life raft for me.

Within hours of posting, I have messages from childhood friends, old neighbours, and people who know people. Every single one of them reassures me that they will find me something, no problem. I can't begin to comprehend this generosity.

I was raised with the assumption that asking for help was a sign of weakness, which could be taken advantage of.

"I'm abroad at the moment, Roselle, but my brother is in Mumbai. I have let him know your situation, and he has lots of connections, he will surely help you. You remember him from our school days, [name]. This is his phone number," says one friend from elementary school.

Another writes: "My parents have a room in their house, but it is far away from where you need to be for your research. You are welcome to use their driver to get to and from work. If there's anything you need while you're there, they said not to hesitate to reach them. Here's their number."

My childhood friend Ronnie, whom I'd grown up with and had gotten into many a childhood scrape with, writes, "Aunty on the sixth floor of our building rents out a room to single women in the city, and her current tenant is about to leave. I've talked to her and she'll give you a good rate because you're our neighbour."

Present tense: you *are* our neighbour. I haven't lived in the neighbourhood or even kept in touch for so long, and still, in the minds of those I have been so desperate to forget, I continue to remain present. Buoyed by this generosity, I decide to stay in the same building I had grown up in. Familiarity with the surroundings will make some things easier.

I haven't been back to Bombay in nearly 15 years. For

many years, I had refused to return to India, but during my trip to Goa five years ago, something shifted for me. India piqued my curiosity. I wanted to know more about the place that birthed me, the one I left behind in adolescence.

My childhood recollections are characterized by my badness: the mischief I would get into, the beatings I endured, being unlovable. Spending my teens and early twenties polishing my perfect Canadian veneer, meant I had to sever all ties to that before-me. I've worked hard over the last few years to integrate those two versions of myself, and excise ideas of myself that are extraneous to who I truly am: neither bad nor perfect.

Yet, the kindness and generosity of my old friends and neighbours fills me with trepidation. I have been taught to question kindness, as if I am unworthy of it. I wrestle with my doubt and trust issues for days leading up to my departure.

En route to the airport, Dustin and I have brunch at our favourite local spot. Potato pancakes because I crave comfort food as I fly off into an adventure filled with uncertainty. We promise to talk every day. The 12-hour time difference means his mornings and my evenings will overlap nicely. We reassure one another with flaccid half-truths that the months of separation will fly by in no time.

My flights take me from Calgary to Toronto, then onward to Brussels, and finally Bombay. For this water baby, being suspended in the air for nearly 20 hours offers a profound liminal space in which to feel my feelings.

I board my flight, and settle into my seat, pulling out a notebook. I am ready to launch into the work, and start by making a list of whom to contact first. I already have a few interviews set up so that I can get started right away. Partway through my list, I become distracted by the cloudscape outside my window.

"Focus, Roselle!"

The self-scolding does nothing to focus me. Instead, it shoves me down a waterslide of anxiety. What if I don't know what I'm doing, and the last few years of foundation laying were for naught? What if I return back from this trip empty-handed, having completely flamed out of the fieldwork?

I spend a significant portion of the flight pondering the razor's edge on which I will have to dance as someone simultaneously inside and outside the community at the heart of my research. A case of Schrödinger's Belonging, if you will.

For so long I have kept the pre-migrant part of myself well-squirreled away, choosing to recall very little of it, and sharing even less. How will I reveal what I find through my research to the academic side of my life without prostrating myself to the ivory tower as a complete phony?

See? I don't belong here. I'll never fully belong because I'll never be fully Canadian. I have all of these weird crunchy bits that underpin who I am.

The internalized sense of shame at my heritage and the perceived sense of Western cultural superiority are both incredibly real. I worry that if I look back into the deep well from whence I came, I will never again be able to turn my back on it as I did when I was a child.

My four-hour layover in Brussels is an invitation to indulge in Anton Berg chocolates. I love the dark chocolate marzipan discs that my father used to bring home from his trips when I was a child, and I have never been able to find them in Canada. A graduate student's budget can always be stretched to find a few sweet luxuries, and I am grateful for that decadence as I board the final leg of my journey to Bombay.

Anton Berg triggers more childhood memories. The good and the bad, the parts I loved and the parts I loathed.

I haven't spoken Hindi in nearly a decade and a half. Will I recall it? I must go see Miss Manju. I hope she isn't upset that I may have forgotten all the Hindi she taught me.

✸

"*Namaste*, Miss."

My five-year-old voice was unsure as I uttered the phrase for the first time, my palms pressed together at my chest. Miss Manju had taught it to me the week before at our first meeting. We didn't say "*namaste*" in our house, and Miss Manju had told me at our introductory meeting that that was how we would greet each other in her house. I was following protocol. Miss Manju was in her kitchen, whipping up a culinary storm.

"Come come," she beckoned. "Wash your hands and then you eat. Do you like *dhokla*?"

"I don't know what that is," I replied, eyeing the delightful fluffy yellow cake-like food that Miss Manju was pointing to. It looked like cake, but it smelled savoury.

I washed my hands and went back to the kitchen.

"Miss, I brought all the things you said. Should I start?"

"No, no. First you must eat. If you fill your stomach first, you'll be able to learn better."

I loved snacks, especially snacks that were unfamiliar. I didn't resist Miss Manju's direction, though I was nervous about not jumping right into my Hindi lessons. Was this going to be some kind of trap? Would I get in trouble for picking snacks over studying?

I came to meet Miss Manju at the urging of my

mother's elder sister, who had met her on a local train and suggested that my mother enroll me in Hindi lessons. While my family was proficient enough in Hindi to get by on the streets of Bombay, it wasn't the *shudh* kind of Hindi that was required in the new fancy boarding school that my cousin had just started. He was three years older than me, and we shared a gift for the intellectual. My aunty thought it wise that I start learning proper Hindi. Miss Manju was actually Dr. Manju. A doctorate in Sanskrit *kavyas*, poetry, had led her to a successful career as an academic. For some odd reason, she had made space in her busy world for me, twice every week, to teach me the bones of a language that she loved.

For nearly a decade, my Hindi tuitions with Miss Manju were constant. Her children became my surrogate siblings. Her husband and his brother became dear uncles whom I could count on for trivia, conversations about current affairs, and discussions about the latest cricket kerfuffle. Miss Manju's next-door neighbours had kids around my age who became friends I played with every week after my Hindi lessons. Miss Manju became my teacher, my mentor, my role model, my surrogate mother, my confidante, my safe place to land. Most of all, in her house, my incessant questions and perpetually-on brain found a home.

At Miss Manju's, I could ask big questions and receive big expansive non-punitive answers. I could explore and wonder and delight in things that were at the outer edges of my world of knowledge.

Once, in a discussion about the *Ramayana*, I enquired about the written origins of this once-oral epic. Miss Manju and her husband, both university professors, offered their knowledge. They couldn't reach a consensus but the next time I was over, they had visited the university library to find me some theories, and had spoken to their colleagues who specialized in the *Ramayana*. All of that so a seven-year-old child would have a thoughtful response to a query.

I am stunned now as I was then that Miss Manju didn't dismiss my questions or me for asking them. Her home was where I learned my questions were valid, my brain was prized, and nurturing it was of immense worth.

One Sunday afternoon, my mother and I were home, watching a movie. The woman on the television had just done something confusing.

"Mama, why did she do that? That doesn't make any sense."

"I'll ask her next time I meet her at church." My mother giggled at her own hilarity.

It took me a few minutes to realize that my mother was mocking me. That she didn't really know the woman in the film. Nor would she meet her at church. Once again, my pesky questions would remain unanswered, and I grew accustomed to the idea that my questioning mind would always be an inconvenience.

Years after I'd left India, when I was deep into graduate studies, I sat for a Hindi language exam at the doctoral level. Upon passing, I messaged Miss Manju the good news:

"You'll be so proud of me! I passed the doctoral Hindi exam!! Thank you so much for teaching me this language. I hope I have made you proud by remembering it all these years."

I wanted her to know that the years of training and love had not been in vain. She responded, expressing pride that I had not let go of the lessons she had instilled in me.

When I walked the stage to receive my doctorate a couple years after that, Miss Manju–whose own daughter had become a leading obstetrics surgeon in India–wrote me a simple line:

"*Vah*! Now both my daughters are doctors. *Shabash, beta.*"

I had been related to Miss Manju by nothing other than her enormous heart, which chose to take me on as a lifelong pupil. She offered regular tutelage to nobody else in all the years I knew her, yet she chose to pour love and energy into shaping me. I will never be able to hold enough gratitude for having been her daughter by choice.

✸

As wave after wave of gratitude washes over me on the flight from Brussels to Bombay, I remember another mother figure that shaped my young life, before the immigration separated us: my godmother, Achie.

Achie is my mother's younger sister and the youngest of Papa's 6 daughters. The year I was born, she'd had a nervous breakdown following the death of her own mother. Following in-patient care for her mental health concerns, she came to live with my parents to support my mother in the impending arrival of a newborn. Achie was the first family member to hold me upon my arrival earthside, and was appointed my godmother at my baptism a few weeks later.

Achie lived with us from my very first day until the day I left India for Canada, some 13 years later. To this day, she calls me "baby." She was my confidante, my protector, my hand-holder until I turned six. On that day, I boldly declared:

"I'm a big girl now, Achie. I can walk alone!"

Walking home from piano lessons, by the Bandra bandstand, the evening ocean breeze sweetened my foray into independence. Achie released her hold on my hand, but walked beside me nonetheless.

As a child, I loved being in the kitchen when Achie cooked. She didn't talk to me like I was a child. Instead, she told me what she was doing and why.

"Always do the *bagaar* nicely, okay? Don't miss out on this. Nice and long."

Her tone was almost scolding as she sauteed onions. I sometimes still hear her caution, especially when I want to skimp on the *bagaar* time!

She told me why it was important to boil the fresh milk that got delivered daily to our door: "Otherwise it will not be good to drink. Boil boil until all the germs die."

She'd skim the cream that rose to the top of the boiling milk, and chase me around the house. When she caught me, the cream would get lathered on my face.

"Achieeeee. Noooo. Ugh." I hated this ritual.

"It's good for your complexion, baby!"

As an adult, I'm inclined to credit my blemish-free skin to this torturous application of gross warm cream, lovingly rubbed by Achie into my juvenile face.

Poverty and unchecked mental illness left Achie with a fourth-grade education, but that didn't inhibit her mastery of music and food. Each day, she'd serenade me—to sleep, to soothe, and just because. My perennial favourites were "*Besame Mucho*" and "Country Roads."

Years later, after moving to Canada, I found a Diana Krall CD at a Costco. My mother couldn't understand why I sobbed to see "*Besame Mucho*" on the track listing. I hadn't heard it in years, and though Krall's version was a passable substitute, it was never the same as Achie's. In my lowest moments, I still let Diana croon to me, wishing for the real thing, and knowing I'll probably never hear it again.

For my whole childhood, Achie wiped my tears, fed me by hand, packed me a hot lunch for school, and picked me up each afternoon. She tolerated my chicanery because I was a rambunctious child. Each evening, she'd take me to the park for playtime.

Where my mother reminded me regularly that she wished she'd had an abortion instead of having me, Achie would remind me often that I was *her* baby.

With shock, I realize on the flight that I haven't seen Achie in so many years. I'm excited to hug her, and eat her food. I don't know what to expect. I'm so sad that I've let this long pass without connecting with her. Though she may have been named my godmother, I know beyond any doubt I have in the existence of a god, that in all the ways that have mattered, she has truly been the only real mother I've ever known.

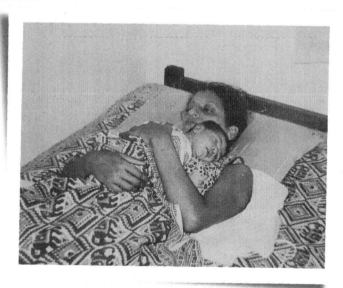

＊

In the last row on the plane, back up against the lavatories, in a middle seat no less, I sob over the rupture of the relationship with my parents. I feel a slithering shame at the failure of being unable to have them love me in the ways that I need. My anger feels righteous when I begin to account for the harms that I've endured in our relationship. Paradoxically, I also often find myself erasing my own experiences so the idea of them can remain protected in my mind. And then, with the kind of depth that one is only able to achieve in the no-timezone space of an enclosed tube hurtling through the air between landmasses, I sleep the sleep of a thousand years.

When I awake, I have returned to the place of my birth.

Insider/Outsider

It's been fifteen years since I left this place. Zooming cars, allergic to both road lines and traffic signals, maintain their status quo. It smells like a memory. A cool breeze floats off the Arabian Sea, whipping my face in the back of the taxi on my way to Bandra, the suburb of Bombay where I will stay for the next few months—the one in which I was born and raised. The flat I'll be living in sits exactly four storeys above the flat that I called home for the first dozen years of life. The same one that permeates my dreams when I dream of "home."

Emotions overwhelm me as the cab pulls onto the street where I'd run throughout my childhood, naughtily peeking into cars parked under old trees, for a glimpse at couples stealing smooches. I'd forgotten how lush this place is, and how eerily quiet it gets at nighttime, save for the vigilant street dogs. I must have taken for granted that I'd always have access to swaying coconut trees and the smell of fresh monsoon rain.

Some things have changed too, as they inevitably do. The old Lion's Club park at the top of the street, where I played every day after school, is gone. In its place is a fancy country club. The swampy abandoned lot across from our compound now holds a public library. The crèche that I went to as a toddler has been replaced by an 8-storey apartment building. Familiar and foreign all at once–like so much of my life.

It is after midnight when I get to the flat. The watchman on duty has to unlock the gates for the cab to enter the compound. In the dim light of the street lamp, I think I recognize him as the watchman from my childhood, the one whose washroom we'd use when we were playing in the compound. He used to tease us and remembered everything about us. It couldn't be though. Too many years have passed, and I am probably just inserting old memories into this new space thanks to a long and draining journey muddled with my penchant for melancholic sentimentality.

The watchman removes my luggage from the taxi. Then he stops in the lobby and looks at me. Really looks at me.

"Baby! *Aap doosare* floor *se hain, nah?*"
(Baby! You're from the 2nd floor, no?)
Shocked, I nod back.
"*Hanh! Mujhe bahut yaad hai. Aap* Canada *gae, nah? Kitne saal ho gae!*"
(Yes! I remember well. You went to Canada, no? So many years have passed!)

He is excited to have recognized me. Still in shock, I smile and nod, and he sends me up in the lift to my new temporary home.

Early the next morning, buoyed by jetlag and excitement, I grab my notebooks and go for a walk. Perhaps I'll get lost in the old neighbourhood so that I can find my place back in it. I pass my old flat, number 22, hoping for a peek inside. Darn, the door is shut. But, the next-door neighbour is at her doorway, buying eggs.

"Roselle, is that you? I heard you were coming home! Come come. Have some tea with me! I'll make us some breakfast."

News travels fast.

"Thanks, Aunty, I'm just heading out for some air, but I'll come visit later."

Even my leisure time is on a strict schedule, and I've slated these next two hours for an orderly exercise in getting reacquainted with the neighbourhood.

The watchman is not at his station when I leave the compound, but the gate is unlocked so I know he is up. I'll catch him on my way back, I think.

As I open the gate, an old familiar voice yells behind me, "Roselle!! Welcome back, man. It's been so long! Good to see you, man!"

It's my friend Ronnie, who'd helped me find accommodations on short notice. His million-watt smile lights up his face as he hugs me. He's much taller than I remembered.

I awkwardly return the hug.

How could he remember me with such fondness when I have tried to erase all that I left behind? How can he respond so generously to my cultural betrayal?

I head for the sea. The salty wind has a way of whipping my head into place. As I walk, I remember. The roads come alive, and I seem to know every turn. I walk past the jogger's park where old men are doing laughing yoga. I laugh with them—the first time I've really laughed in weeks. I catch a whiff of dried fish—an olfactory delicacy.

I trip in a pothole and chuckle. Some things don't change. A bright red B.E.S.T double-decker bus drives by, its trail of fumes enveloping me in a wave of nostalgia. All of this seems somehow familiar. How do I still know this place I've tried so hard to forget?

Ambling through Chimbai, my nana Cecelia's ancestral village, and past the *banya*, I remember my old friend, the woman with matted hair and lavender body wash. Further down the way, now on St. Paul's Road, I pass by the building where my old uncle friend lived—the one who quizzed me about times tables and once gave me a chocolate bar. I'm certain that they have both passed away by now, and if not, surely they would not remember me. I can't fathom explaining to them the impact they had on my young life.

Lost in memories, I find myself at St. Andrew's Church, the place where so many generations of my family have been baptized, married, and buried. I make a mental note to visit the family gravesite, almost bumping into an older woman, hurrying somewhere.

"Oops, sorry Aunty."

She smiles kindly, and a flash of recognition hits me.

"Excuse me, Aunty. Are you Dr. Marie?"

"Yes, I am."

"Doctor, you might not remember me. My name is Roselle Gonsal–"

"Roselle!" Dr. Marie interrupts. "How could I forget you, my girl? I was the one who brought you into this world. I will always remember you."

She hugs me.

"I'm so happy to see you, my girl. I'm happy you've come home for a visit. I will pray for you."

As suddenly as she appeared, Dr. Marie hurries off to morning Mass.

I'm stunned. Everything about this place feels surprising, as though the version I had demonized and rejected was illusory at best. Something Dr. Marie said about coming home for a visit really stood out to me. This place *does* feel like a long-forgotten home, and yet, I'm also missing home–*my* home. The one I've made with Dustin and Zeke. I rush off to a cell phone shop to find a way to call home.

✶

"Hello? Hello? Babes, can you hear me?"

Sputtering crackle on the other end. Gah! This is frustrating. I should be able to dial a number and get through, but instead the last three days have been an adventure in finding a SIM card and buying a new phone because my Canadian one isn't playing well in the Indian telecom sandbox. I haven't spoken to Dustin since I got to Bombay, and while the romance of reacquainting myself with my childhood home is still in full bloom, pangs of homesickness and culture shock are also beginning to set in.

Does every immigrant feel this dissonance of being in one home while simultaneously yearning for the other?

Everywhere I go in this first week, friends and family are exuberant.

"Welcome home!"

"It's been so long since you've been home."

"Must be so good to be home."

It feels really good to be back in a home space that my heart is beginning to recall. And still, I regularly trip into linguistic potholes:

"This phone that I brought from home doesn't work here. Uh…I mean, Canada, I brought it from Canada."

"I'm looking for a place to buy some pre-made meals. Do you know where I should go? At home, uh I mean, in Canada, we have them in the grocery stores."

In a single motion, I have both come home and left home.

"I can hear you." Dustin's beautiful familiar voice breaks through the crackle.

I could cry at the intensity of hearing something that feels like a safe harbour. It's noon on my end and midnight on his, so we don't chat for very long. The call itself is like an exhale, brief and necessary. We plan to chat again in a few hours, when he's on his way to work.

Navigating timezones is yet another golden thread woven through the universal migrant's experience, bridging not only space but also time.

Each of my days in Bombay is bookended by a phone call with Dustin. In between are research interviews, library trips, visits with community members, friends, neighbours, loved ones, and new acquaintances. Each interview has me enquiring about their identities, listening to understand how they see themselves fit into the broader context of what it means to be Indian. In each conversation, I feel increasingly more validated in the rupture of my own identity: a vestige of colonial exercises, fully a part of, and simultaneously apart from, the Indian cultural landscape.

"Oh my goodness," I gush to Dustin at the end of each day. "You won't believe what I heard today…"

Our twice-daily calls tether my two worlds–a daily reporting back of real-time data collection, to a person who sees me more clearly than anyone I've ever known, and who holds each new piece of information as a precious slice of a much larger story.

Every so often, he chimes in: "Hey, that sounds similar to what so-and-so said a few days ago. Remember?"

On one call, Dustin says: "That is incredible that you were able to go there with them. You would never have that insight if they didn't trust you and if you didn't have a deep understanding of what they were telling you. This is why you're able to tell their story, and yours. You get it in your bones."

Long before the tedious process of anthropologically coding my research interviews for themes and patterns, Dustin is providing me with an outside observer's lens on the connectivity of lived experiences that I am so privileged to engage with here.

When I finally begin writing the 400 pages of my doctoral dissertation, a year from now, I will think back on this time in India, and the duality of my presence in the community: at once a researcher and observer, while also a member and participant. I will be compelled to dedicate an entire chapter of my dissertation to this interstitial occupation of being an insider/outsider. I exist on the backslash that separates the two worlds.

The academic ivory tower as a whole, and in particular the practice of modern Western ethnographic research, pioneered by the likes of Malinowski, Evans-Pritchard, and Boaz, assumes that the Western gaze on the "other" is a perfectly reasonable exercise in objectivity. Examining a community to which I have deep lived connectivity challenges this academic illusion of objectivity, and I will be forced to justify my ability to remain objective, rational, removed, or whatever other condescendingly paternalistic adjective fits here.

While in Bombay, I am too consumed with the joy of

being in the community, attending feast day celebrations, asking questions, enjoying home-cooked food, and finding parts of myself that have been dormant for too long. I have neither the time nor the need to concern myself with how all of this will translate to my academic work.

While objectivity might be the illusory cloak of the privileged, separating one from the other, it is devoid of the gifts of investment, embodiment, finding one's place within one's matter of inquiry. The exercise of having to justify my knowledge and academic rigor simply because of the body and place into which I was born, does not sit well with me. Why am I expected to *know* less because I understand more? It seems foolish that knowledge and understanding would be at loggerheads with each other.

"I can't wait to tell this story in my dissertation," I tell Dustin one evening. "I think being here, actually being here–not just studying–is going to be what will deepen my work."

My heart is thawing after a long winter. The buds haven't yet unfurled, but the tree is illuminated by the glow of the emerging green.

"I think my work after this is to be a bridge builder." The words only find heft once they leave my lips.

"On one hand, nobody in my academic world has any embodied insight into this world. On the other, people here see life in the West as some kind of Promised Land. I think I want to be a cultural translator, so that people like me can be seen, even when we fall in between two worlds."

The words tumble from me, purpose-driven yet tentative. I have no idea what I've put into motion, but something akin to peace is present in the realization that while I'm both at home and also away from home, I can find something of beauty in the space between.

✴

I have tried so hard these past 15 years to untie myself from this place, but it continues to remember me. It remains so that I have both, the freedom to forget, and also to return, ready to re-remember who I am.

In the lobby, I spot the watchman.

"Ah, baby! *Aaj bohut jaldee nikal gae!*"

(Baby! You left early today!)

I nod.

"Watchman, *aap mujhe yaad karte ho? Aap mere bach-chpan se yahaan hee hain, nah?*"

(Watchman, you remember me? You've been here since my childhood, no?)

He nods, his face registering shock as I speak to him in Hindi. I am equally shocked at the fluency with which these words fly out of my mouth.

"*Aap kaise ho? Aapka patnee aur bachche abhee bhee gaanv mein hain? Voh kaise hain?*"

(How are you? Are your wife and children still in the village? How are they?)

My Hindi tumbles out from a long unopened vault. The past 15 years of trying to forget, pretending I don't know this second native tongue is futile against the sheer force of being seen, recognized, remembered.

His face is radiant in being remembered by me in return. I remember his family too, for whom he works so hard to provide. As a child I felt so sad for his kids, who only got to see him once every few months. Once, they'd come to visit him in our building, and we played together as children do, without care for class or social standing or the triflings of what keeps us segregated as adults.

"Baby! *Main aapko kaise bhool sakata hoon? Yeh aapka ghar hai. Tum ghar aa gae ho.*"

(Baby! How could I forget you? This is your home. You have come home.)

I smile, grateful for this moment between me and a man I will always only know as "watchman," and to whom I will eternally be "baby."

Ch-ch-ch-choices

"You're not going to believe this!" I'm excited to share my news with Dustin. "Aunty got me a meeting with that professor I was telling you about. Next Sunday afternoon."

One of the world's foremost scholars on the Goan community lives in Bombay, and I am determined to connect with her as part of my work here. Retired from her academic roles, now in her 80s, I tried contacting her for months before arriving.

Email, telephone, and all other forms of contemporary communication fell short of connecting me to her. So I employed some old-world tactics. Like the world's best game of six degrees of separation, someone at a friend's church knows someone who knows the emeritus professor and, as is the case with all of my work in community, has offered me the generous gift of creating a connection.

The professor's church parish is quite a distance away from where I am located in the city, so I attend Sunday Mass there prior to our meeting. As is the case with all of my research interlocutors, she insists on feeding me. A Sunday post-Mass lunch is the pinnacle of all meals, in my humble opinion. Having appeased both a spiritual cleansing and a communal connection, the food tastes that much more delicious.

As we eat and chat, the professor enquires about my roots.

"This is a very enticing research project you have embarked upon, Roselle. Tell me, how did you come to this work? Where are you coming from?"

By now, I am quite practiced at the elevator pitch of who I am in the context of my relations and ancestors, and I add that my Papa moved to Bombay in 1918. That he made his home, where my mother and her siblings grew up, in *Dhobi Talao*, in South Bombay.

"Oh, you know when I was a child, my piano teacher lived there too—he was a very respected man."

"Oh wow. My grandfather was a music teacher too. He was a military bandmaster, but after the British left, he used to do concerts and give music tuition on the side. His name was Francisco Florencio Menezes."

She stares at me, eyes wide, morphing into a teenager right before me. She stands slowly from the dining table, and picks a thin book about Goan pioneers in Bombay from her bookshelf.

"This is one of the first books that I wrote," she says, flipping it open.

Handing me the book, open to page 42, the professor watches as I read. It is about my Papa, his music, his band, and the impact that he had on the music scene in the city of Bombay, complete with photographs of him and his bandmates.

"For the granddaughter of Mr. Menezes, ask me anything and I'm happy to help you."

This esteemed academic would go on to champion my research, and I remain eternally grateful for her guidance. As I process my connection to this scholar sitting across the lunch table from me, each connected to a man now long gone, I am in awe. Papa could not have fathomed the ripple effects of his work on my life, but decades after leaving me, he has found a way to set me up in a good way.

It's difficult for me to reconcile that other people's choices have had such profound impacts on my life. It is wondrous to consider that my choices will have those same long lasting impacts on lives I will never know.

I leave the professor's home, thanking her profusely, and promising to send her a copy of my completed dissertation. I haven't spoken to my parents in all the time that I've been in Bombay. I wonder what my mother would think of today's meeting. I wonder if her resentment of me would overshadow any joy she might feel at this serendipity.

My mother's love of me has always been full of "should haves." Regrets for choices she didn't make. Resentment for choices she felt I'd stolen from her. Like resentment—which Malachy McCourt famously said is akin to taking poison and expecting the other person to die—my mother's regrettable choices have poisoned any semblance of a relationship we might have had.

"I should have stayed in the convent. Then I wouldn't have had to deal with you."

"I should have done what my sister did with the coat hanger, then I wouldn't have to put up with this."

"I shouldn't have brought you to Canada. Now you

think you know more than me."

"I should play you that song 'No Charge.' Some mothers charge their children for all these things I do for you for free."

There's a scene in the miniseries *Little Fires Everywhere*, where Elena, a well-off white woman, chastises her maid: "In my book, a good mother puts her daughter's needs before her own. A good mother makes good choices. She doesn't drag a child from town to town, school to school. She doesn't smoke marijuana or just leave her daughter to fend for herself. And she really doesn't leave a baby alone in the cold, in front of a fire station."

Mia, the Black woman who works in Elena's home, spits back with biting elocution: "You didn't make good choices, you *had* good choices."[1]

This single line has remained with me since I first watched it.

Choices often seem like the inevitable culs-de-sac of what's available. My mother could have chosen either one of the Catholic sacraments of service: Holy Order or Holy Matrimony. When she was dismissed from the convent, the former became unavailable. The latter became, in her mind, her only option. She chose to have a child, but she didn't choose the child she was given. If one's choices are merely micropoints on the top of a pyramid of unresolved trauma and pain, are those actually real choices?

The spate of choices available in my life have been created by the privilege of financial security. My personality has had the ability to flourish unhindered by the shame of bone-deep poverty that my mother experienced. My physical health has benefited from childhood nutrition, and access to regular medical and dental care. The social

1   Little Fires Everywhere. 2020. Season 1, Episode 4, "The Spider Web." Directed by Lynn Shelton. Aired March 25, 2020 on Amazon Prime.

determinants of health continue to benefit those of us who already have access to so much.

I am the benefactor of a smorgasbord of choices that make a good life–a smorgasbord that I imagine my mother longed for.

It is only through the benefit of hindsight, compassion, and many many hours of therapy that I have been able to see this duality of my mother's yearnings, and hold them tenderly alongside the harms that she has inflicted upon my life. Two disparate things can hold true simultaneously.

✻

Privilege illuminates choices for us. Marginalization invisiblizes them. In many ways, our choices choose us, through accidents of birth and circumstance. Quantum mechanics suggests that there is no such thing as free will. Choice is an illusion, with each choice presenting an option between A or B. The current choice is itself predicated upon the countless As and Bs that have been presented all the way back to the start of life itself. Regardless of where our choices present themselves, choosing is our opportunity to impact our world, sometimes for generations to come.

Papa chose to remarry. It was unheard of for a widower of his generation to raise three girls alone. His choice in Omai kept with tradition and the family's focus on status and propriety. It also meant that a young woman, herself not yet a full-fledged adult, would never be able to offer Papa's eldest daughters the kind of mothering they might have needed. All three girls ended up in boarding schools, resentful of Papa's new family. Omai was the villain in their story.

Already impoverished, Papa and Omai chose to have six more children. I use "chose" here tentatively as I don't imagine Omai had much choice in this situation. What I do know is that by the time she'd had the first four of her children, she had had enough. She *did* choose to take medication to induce chemical abortions for subsequent pregnancies: medication that didn't work, and instead resulted in detrimental health outcomes for her youngest two. So, in an age and place where reproductive choice wasn't an option, Omai chose to introduce her own daughters to birth control pills when they came of age in the 1970s. Her own choices, or lack thereof, yielded a perspective that compelled her to offer her children a different choice.

Our choices, whether chosen by or for us, offer us a relational opportunity to choose them as a conduit for impact on this world. As I hail a rickshaw to take me back to Bandra after lunch with the professor, I wonder what life would have been like had my mother chosen to understand and nurture me instead of meeting me with resistance, resentment, and rejection? What would my life have been like had she chosen *me*?

✻

Simultaneously excited and saddened, I try to capture the intensity of the day's synchronistic encounter on my call to Dustin. "Such a small world," I keep saying over and over, awash in disbelief at meeting someone who actually knew my Papa–out in the world, not just as the patriarch of our family. He lived, and he made a difference, not only to me as a small child, but also to the elderly woman I got to share a meal with today. We both held him in the same vaulted space in our memories.

Those memories are all that connect me to Papa now.

"I'm going to grab a copy of her book," I tell Dustin. "I want to remember Papa as she captured him in her research."

I feel the weight of grief as I remember that only a few weeks ago I lost the only talisman that connected me to my Papa: the hand-sized piece of a red roof tile that I found five years earlier at his childhood home.

Dustin asks gently, "There's no way for you to go to Goa and find another one, eh?"

"I can't! Funds are super tight, and I'm really missing home now. I just want to come home."

The wear and tear of displaced living is starting to catch up with me. Even in finding new routines, I miss my old ones.

"Also, I wouldn't even know where to go if I went to Goa."

I am trying to convince Dustin, though I am quite possibly mostly trying to assuage myself.

"It's not like I have an address or anything. I think I just have to make peace with the fact that the tile is gone, but maybe a good way to look at it is that it got replaced by my connection with the professor and finding Papa in her work."

I'm not buying my own consolation prize.

Loss weighs me down. My voice is soft and low to salve the unbearable sorrow of speaking this pain too loudly:

"I think the tile is gone for good."

Another world is not only possible, she is on her way.
On a quiet day, I can hear her breathing.

—Arundhati Roy
"World Social Forum" Speech, 2003

Repair

2018

Reconnection

"Mom, it's really difficult to have a conversation with you if you keep making everything about you. There's no room for me to even get a word in edgewise. It's like you don't want to hear what I have to say."

All of our conversations over the last five years have found their way to this same, frustrating point.

"This is just the way I was created. Why is it so hard for you to accept me as I am?"

"It's fine that that's how you are, mom. But it's hard to engage with you when there's no room for me in our relationship."

"So anytime someone has a flaw, you just crucify them?"

"I'm not trying to be judgemental, mom. I just want to feel like I am being heard. Is that something we can do together?"

"You know, you only have one family in this life. Everything is about family, and here you are just treating me like garbage. You'll remember this when I'm gone."

"Mom, I don't think you're hearing me at all. You know I love my family. I just want to be respected and not treated abusively."

"All we have is love. We must keep love alive."

Our conversations are discordant and futile, but I keep trying.

Every time we clash, I retreat and re-emerge with some new idea on how to approach my relationship with my folks.

It's been five years since the fabric of our fragile relationship tore irrevocably. I tried hard to reconnect with them when I got back from my research trip, wanting to unpack how we got to that point. My efforts were met with denial that any harm had occurred, and worse, that I was making it all up. As if I didn't have dozens of poison-filled emails to validate what I had experienced.

After every failed attempt, I take time to lick my wounds. Then, once some time has passed, I try again.

Each time, I convince myself that the potential our relationship has outweighs the harm. The grief of these torturous efforts compound over time.

I procrastinate putting ink to paper so much. I wonder if deep down I'm afraid that if I start pouring out, the anguish will never cease...that not enough ink in the world could do justice to the tears and rage I feel.

I wonder too, if on paper, I'm supposed to be joyful - joyous - grateful for all the goodness in my life. And yes...I have built myself a beautiful life - a happy joy-filled one. But this in spite of all that has been stolen from me - all that I never had...joy on top of such deep grief.

F said to me today - "Anger, sat with, reveals herself to be grief."

And grief it is.

Grief for a family of birth that didn't want me -
At least not the me that I am or was -
Grief that I never fit into the mould they made for me -
Grief that I couldn't make them love me -
Grief that that will never be a possibility -
Grief that their vision of me taints MY vision of me -
Grief that they'll never know me in my fullness, or at all...I think i'm a good person to know -
Grief for a warm and caring mother - or lack thereof
Grief for a present and interested father - or agin, lack thereof
Grief for relation lost with my brother
Grief that in our immigrant experience, they untethered me from so much good -
Grief for the shame that they instilled in me - shame of culture, of heritage, of my very skin -
Grief for loss of ties to language space and place, stories, recipes -
Grief for the years of violence and abuse I endured - physical, psychological, emotional -
Grief that I may never fully heal those wounds -
Grief that every person I love or who loves me will be touched by the tentacles of that trauma -
Grief that trust will never come easily -
Grief that running will always come too easily -

Grief
Grief
Grief
Grief

I worry that I could fill up this entire journal. This entire room. This entire house. This entire world.

And yet...I keep wanting to try...

If I try just the right way, I will unlock in them an ability to see me, to hear me, to love me.

*

Years from now, the whole world will grind to a halt when hit by a global pandemic.

A few weeks before the world shuts down, I will start a new job at a consulting firm. Working from home will mean spending more time with Zeke, who by then will be in his twilight years. Zeke will snore gently on my lap through virtual meetings and unmuting myself, as snow turns to rain. The first few weeks will be an introvert's delight: I will bake bread, make seasonally inappropriate knitwear, and start hand-drawing a recipe book. With almost no in-person contact, I will watch governmental updates every evening, and my CBD intake will increase to keep up with my anxiety.

Queues will form outside grocery stores. Shelves will be bare of pantry and toiletry staples. The air will be prickly, like the stillness before a raging thunderstorm.

Then, a Black man's final few minutes of life will be captured on a shaky cell phone camera, and in the span of 72 hours, the world will go from being tensely still to feeling like the inside of a snow globe being shaken by a rambunctious child.

A social reckoning of the anti-Black racism that permeates our societies will break through the permafrost of social palsy. My career in the professional landscape of inclusion will have been, until that point, an undervalued and underpaid vocation, driven by my own sense of knowing that we can build a better world than the one we have: the one in which a Black man can be lynched in the public square, and be just another part of the news cycle.

It will be a historically perfect storm. Twiddling our thumbs at home, and doing virtual yoga, terrified of an undetectable virus, we will no longer be able to ignore the malignancy of social oppression.

Masked, angry, and crying hot tears, I will scream "Black Lives Matter" in Calgary's Olympic Plaza. Matter is the barest damn minimum. The whole world will have shut down for a virus, but the merry-go-round of white supremacy and anti-Black racism will continue, with its many tentacles permeating our society, our workplaces, our laws, our schools, our words, our actions, our thoughts.

As my grief and helplessness percolate in those raw days of the summer of 2020, I will feel voiceless to rage against a machine designed to silence voices that sound a certain way. My helplessness will feel all-encompassing in regards to ensuring the psychological, social, emotional, and physical safety of my Black loved ones. On more than one occasion, after a long day of intense virtual meetings, I will find myself in the fetal position on the floor. Nothing past that will feel in my control.

Externally, the murder of George Floyd will catalyze the systemic and strategic work of inclusion to deafening volumes. The intersection of my expertise and experience will never be more in demand. On the inside, the toll of these conversations on my physical being will become more palpable by the day. I am not a Black person and so will never understand the sheer magnitude of oppression that Black bodies experience in our world. As a person whose body holds multiple intersections of marginalized identities, it is not always easy to sit in the messy business of fixing a system that I didn't design or break.

Helpless and burnt out, my rage will boil over in endless tears, and I will yearn for maternal comfort, for soothing balm to treat my wounded heart, for something that in those dark moments I won't be able to do or be for myself. News of people succumbing to the virus in record numbers, especially in India, will weigh on my heart. I will worry about the well-being of my parents, to whom I haven't been connected for some time. I will wonder whether the bottle is dad's solace. Will the church be that for my mother?

Once again I will try to reconnect after years of silence between us.

Our first call will be tentative. I will tell my mother that I want to know her as she is today. I imagine that she may not be the same person as the mother in my memory and wounds. She will say she wants that too.

My mother will tell me all about her volunteering at a local hospital, to support the inundated healthcare workers with non-medical duties.

"You know, I'm an essential worker now. They even gave me an award for exceptional service. It was in the newspaper."

"That's amazing, mom. I'm proud of you!"

In the two-hour phone call, she will not ask me one question about my life.

When vaccines become available and travel once again quasi-acceptable, a business trip will take me close to where my mother lives.

"Hey mom. I'm going to be in Toronto for a meeting in a couple weeks. I'm wondering if you'd be open to having dinner with me. I'm happy to fly in a day early or leave a day later if something in those days works on your end?"

"I can't. I'm very busy volunteering and don't want to move my shifts."

I will bawl in the parking lot of a Jiffy Lube, grieving over what my heart yearns for.

✻

Sometimes months go by between my attempts to re-connect with my parents. Sometimes, the months stretch into years. The last attempt left me inconsolable, on my therapist's couch, wailing at being so unlovable.

"If the two people who are meant to love me most in this world see me as broken, unlovable, a bad seed, then maybe that's true?"

I pose my half-question, hoping to be proven wrong in my hypothesis.

Every attempt I have made to reconnect with my parents is built on the hope that they might someday revise their opinion of me. Maybe if I work harder, achieve more, am thinner, contort my very being. Maybe.

Hope is a seductive drug.

So, I try.

"I called my parents today."

"Oh yea? How did it go?"

Dustin is always so kind every time I try something new to repair the relationship with my parents, to find a way to earn their love, to be everything they want me to be.

The me that I am has no desire to obfuscate any part of how abundantly I show up in the world; I take up space, and I've always been alright with that reality. On the other hand, my parents' desire for a daughter has always been for one who melts away all aspects of herself that don't enmesh with their lives. One who is subservient, less questioning, less self-assured. Surely, I can find a balance between these two options? A happy medium might stop them from punishing me for being…well, me.

Dustin never criticizes my foolhardy attempts, which at this point seem akin to banging my head against the wall. I think he understands my need to try, but I'm embarrassed to tell him about my latest foray nonetheless.

"How are they doing?" Dustin inquires.

"I think they were happy that I called. I'm going to take it super slow this time. I'm going to try just meeting them where they're at. I don't need anything from them emotionally or otherwise, so I can just be surface level, and take it slow."

I don't know whom I'm trying to convince, him or me. Dustin gives no indication that he's swayed one way or another. He just takes in my news as if it's brand new information.

A few weeks pass, and I continue to keep my promise to myself to keep things light in my weekly calls, despite my parents' desire to race past this into a resumption of us as a perfect, closely-knit family. If I don't need anything from them, then I can't be let down. I try limiting our calls to an hour. But in a relationship where boundaries have always been broken, I am often unable to extricate myself for three or four hours at a time. I end the calls depleted from the unidirectional give of energy.

After one such call, Dustin checks in with me.

"I didn't say very much," I say. "They didn't ask how I'm doing. They just told me about what's happening in their lives. Apparently my cousin is getting married. We've been invited."

Dustin is intrigued. He's always wanted to go to India with me. Maybe this will be an opportunity to integrate healing into my parental relationship in the same way that I'd done in my relationship with India five years earlier.

"Where would we stay?" he asks.

"My parents said we're welcome to stay with them at their flat in Bombay, and then at their villa in Goa."

"Oh wow, that's so generous. Do you want to go?"

This round of experimental reconnection with my parents has been relatively positive. I'm not getting much out of the relationship, but in a dynamic that hasn't ever had room for me anyway, this seems like a net neutral outcome. They've extended this generous offer, and maybe as a show of good faith, I should take them up on it.

"I think I can get the time off work. Let's go!"

I can hardly believe that I'm getting the opportunity to take my beloved Dustin to the place that bore me and shaped so much of who I've become. I am bursting with joy at all the places I want to show him, and all the stories that will now have context for him. To top it off, we will be in Goa for a milestone anniversary—five years together. What a cool way to celebrate the life we've built.

Plans for the fortnight-long trip commence in full force. We get passports, visas, and vaccinations. The plan is to spend a week in Bombay, for my cousin's wedding. Then, off to Goa and the beach! We make itineraries for places we want to see and things we want to do. One afternoon, as we're listing all the sites in Goa that we want to see, Dustin asks a question that will have some big ripples.

"How hard would it be for us to get to your Papa's house? We should try and get you another tile."

Funhouse Mirrors and Trusted Reflections

Dustin giggles and then bursts into full-blown laughter as we walk past the old men doing their daily laughing yoga outside the jogger's park in Bandra. We shush each other, and hurry away from the group, giggling like naughty children. The tender pinks and blues of the dawn sky are just starting to take shape on the Bandra seawall.

Jet lag has us awake, and we head down to Carter Road to take a walk that echoes the one I took by myself five years ago. Today though, instead of being weighed down by shame, I'm buoyed by pride at showing my beloved the stomping grounds of my childhood.

"That's my piano teacher's house. I didn't like her very much. Oh, and there's Betty Vincent's house, where I did elocution every week."

Remembering every turn in the road, I point excitedly to the landmarks that shaped my young life. I'm not sure whether it means anything to Dustin, these plot points on a voyage that someone else charted. Yet, he is gleeful in our exploration. We stop at a *chai* stand, and order a round of *kadak chai* to dispel the cobwebs of international travel and put us into this new place.

"You code switch in about twelve different ways when you're here." Dustin's observation is tinged with awe, "Like, at least three languages, and then different accents and tones depending on whom you're speaking to."

As we sip our tea, I feel a dormant lick of shame crawl its way up my neck and shoulders. There is no hiding from Dustin here. I am all of me with him in this place because together they demand that I remove all veils. I cannot exist solely in English in this multilingual place. I automatically mirror the accents of the people around me, giving my English a lilting flair that falls somewhere between native Indian and naturalized Canadian.

In Canada, whenever someone picks up on vestiges of my Indian accent, it is accompanied by a semi-accusation of being foreign, as if I have bamboozled them to my true identity. It often feels like a gotcha moment, and I feel embarrassed for reasons unknown.

As I begin to dismiss Dustin's observation, I am stopped by his look of admiration. "It's amazing! You just swim in and out of these different ways of communicating. It's seamless. We don't do that in the West. We have one way of talking and that's the end of that. Here, it's like you're shaped to be a cultural translator."

By letting Dustin, a touchstone of my life in the new world, have a view into me in the old world, I've created a bridge I cannot uncross. One that demands that I be valiantly unerased because there is no place to hide the parts of myself that I worry might make me less palatable. There is an undeniable freedom in bridging my worlds through the eyes of someone who sees me, and with whom I have created a safe world.

Taken aback, my eyes well up with unexpected tears, and I'm overcome by a wave of gratitude.

For so long I held firm to the idea that my accent, the languages I speak, the code switching I undertake in my day to day, albeit unintentional, are something to be embarrassed about. Yet, the person who knows me best and whom I love most, not only believes that these things do *not* make me inferior, but actually give me the ability to engage in the worlds that I do, swimming easily in and out of waters in which I do not always fully belong.

✳

In the debilitating days after being fired from my job for daring to speak truth to power, I started working out three times a week with my friend Jean. Between my training for a half-marathon, and her love of our sadistic yoga teacher, we spent many hours sweating out our woes.

"I don't even know how to process this, Jean." We were enjoying a post-workout burrito. "Like, what did I do that was so wrong? Is it wrong to have spoken up about being treated unfairly?"

Jean and I had been round and round this carnival ride a few times now. I feared that what the organization had told me when they let me go was true: that I was not a fit, that I was challenging and disrespectful.

"Roselle, life is like going through a gallery of funhouse mirrors. Some will be true reflections and some will be distorted to exaggerate your worst perceptions of yourself." Jean held tender space for my heart and fears, "Learn which mirrors to trust, and ignore the rest. They make up lies that you'll believe because we all have insecurities."

In those harrowing days of feeling underwater, unable to understand how I'd gotten to this point, I was deafened by my worst fears: that I am incompetent, incapable, an imposter.

Jean reminded me to surround myself with trusted reflections of who I truly am.

This practice of showing my vulnerabilities to those around me, and trusting them to reflect truth back at me, is something that I have found profound strength in, although it has also been really scary. I was raised to believe that I couldn't trust anyone, that no one would love me because I was too much: too Indian, too bossy, too untamed. I had worked hard to craft my illusion of perfection. I've had to work twice as hard to dismantle it all.

I had been presented with a fresh opportunity for this when I moved to Calgary in my mid-twenties. It was early September and Emma had just walked into our shared apartment in graduate housing:

"Hello!!!" she sang as she entered. "I'm your Emma!"

I'm guessing she wanted to say that she was my new roommate, Emma, but I was immediately endeared by her sweet introduction. In our year of living together, we witnessed each other at our best and worst.

One night, close to midnight, there was an urgent knock at the door.

"Hey Roselle. The police are here for you."

I thought Emma was playing a prank on me. She had once covered my bedroom door in rows of toilet paper, so it looked like I was blocked in my room when I opened my bedroom door the next morning.

"Yea, I'm sure they are. Did I rob a bank?"

"No, for real. Come here!"

Standing in the doorway of our mostly-beige apartment, were two police officers.

"Are you Roselle Gonsalves?"

"I am. What is this about?"

"Your mother called us to do a safety check on you. Could you please call her back? She's been trying to get in touch with you."

"I spoke to her this afternoon. Like, I literally spoke to her six hours ago. I don't understand why she'd call you?"

My bewilderment was second only to my absolute horror and embarrassment, as I tried to find a reason for why my mother would call the police on me. What the actual f*$k?

"Just call her and tell her you're safe."

"It's after 2 am her time."

"She said she'd be awake."

I shut the door to the police officers, wanting to melt into the gray grout on the tiled entryway.

"Come, let's go have a smoke, and clear your head."

Emma guided me outside to the crisp night air. No words, no judgement. Just tenderness and love.

Deflated, I told her everything. How bad things were as a child, how shitty my parents had become over the last few years, and about how I didn't know how to be loved by them.

I shared with Emma the pain that I had never shared with anyone else. She held me with grace. When I walked in her wedding party a few years later, I wept at the beauty of bearing witness to each other's lives. She remains forever *my* Emma.

Cracking myself open to Emma made me want to

be honest with others in my life too.

Like Annie, who'd been a dear sister-friend since we'd met years earlier at an immersive French program in rural Quebec, and whom I'd been ashamed to talk to when the relationship with my parents nosedived into oblivion. For so long I had pretended it was a perfect relationship.

"My dear Annie. I'm so sorry that I've been so terrible at keeping in touch these last few months."

Through shame and fear of rejection, I wrote her the world's longest email. She's a kickass lawyer and I thought I needed to show her as much evidence as I could so she would believe me.

Within minutes, she had responded with an email that I still pull up and read when my demons slither back

New Message

From: Annie

Subject RE: Hello & I'm SO Sorry!!!

First let me say I love you, I love you, I love you.

From the time I met you till right this moment finishing this email, I have always known [sic] what an amazing sister friend I have in you. You are one of the smartest, strongest, most beautiful souls I know.

I am so sorry for the shit you've had to put up with but so grateful you've had Dustin's support (remember when I said he's like a manifestation of all the goodwill and love you put out in the world) yup, mmhmm, I called that.

We have much to catch up on, but I'll end with two things:

1. You are so loved.
2. The word family means many things, it's not just the people who you came through, it's also the people you choose. Sometimes the ones who are supposed to love us the most don't. But you have a family that loves you, they go by the names of Dustin, Annie, Louise, Damian, Jean, Emma, and that's all the names I can remember, but you get the idea.

I love you so much, let me know when you're free to talk, xoxo :)

In the smallest darkest corners of me, I still doubt my worthiness of such sweet love. The poison pill sits in a deep cavern, where I rarely go now. Increasingly, the light shines through.

The more I open up to people around me, the more I am met with kindness and generosity, and over the years, I've had a handful of close friends who have held me steadfastly as I've removed the barricades to my heart.

Like Jean and Lindsey, with whom I've spent at least one long weekend on the land each summer for the last decade. Regardless of anything else going on in our lives, we sit around the fire, under stars, psilocybin in effect, sharing our hearts. Accolades don't matter here, just who I am at my core. They tease me affectionately, and I trounce them at bocce ball. There is no judgement, just love, and even if we don't talk for weeks or months, I am guaranteed one perfect summer weekend of reconnection each year. I never feel too much out on the land. My laugh isn't too loud, my jokes aren't too weird. I can just be, and count on my friends to be themselves in all their glory as well. This annual ritual nourishes me.

It is the same kind of nourishment that has been offered to me by my beloved Louise and Emmanuel, who for almost 20 years have offered me refuge. I first began retreating to their home in Waterloo when I was a student in Toronto and the relationship with my parents began fracturing beyond my abilities to repair it. Louise and Emmanuel were whom I first introduced Dustin to, because they've always been "family." Regardless of where life has taken me, I know that with them, I always have a bed to sleep on, pajamas to don, and hearty meals to eat. They never questioned my need to escape. Instead, they gave me hope when I had none, been my family when I felt orphaned, championed my wins, and sheltered me.

"You always have a home here with us," they tell me every time I visit. I know beyond knowledge that this is true.

This knowing, of being loved and cherished, is overwhelming at times.

I see now the wisdom of the words that Ana wrote in my high school yearbook, that year we all went our separate ways. I hold deep gratitude for all the gifts of relationship that have come my way. They have nourished and enriched me, both during the time in my life when they were active. Perhaps more so in perpetuity.

In relinquishing the illusion of perfection, in choosing to trust myself and the loved ones around me, rather than the poison of what I'd been incepted with as a child, I have breathed life into the term "chosen family."

I am pulled out of my sentimental reverie as Dustin and I cross a busy street in Bandra. Something across the street has caught his eye.

"Let's get a newspaper! Which one?"

"We got the *Times of India* every morning when I was growing up. And then at noon-time, we got the *Mid-Day*, which is kind of like our *Sun*."

Dustin is in awe of the number of languages represented at the newsstand.

"Does everyone speak and read multiple languages?"

I shrug. I have no data to back up my affirmative response, but my lived experience would suggest that bilingualism is the bare minimum for most folks around whom I grew up. Many of us also have regional tongues that augment our polyglottery.

Our morning walk takes us to the boardwalk, where we watch birds pick at dried fish. The *machchiwallis* don't pay the birds too much mind. There's enough for them to share. Besides, it's time for the boats to go out for the day's haul.

As life comes up to full volume around us, Dustin reaches for my hand.

"*Chalo*! Let's go!"

Over the years, he's picked up a few key phrases in the languages that I hold, and we use them regularly. An aunty walking past us does a double take at the image of this blue-eyed white-skinned man saying "*chalo*" with such nonchalance, like it were part of his everyday vernacular. She giggles and hurries past.

"What are we losing out on because we only have one language to filter all the information in the world through?"

Dustin poses the question to the air as we walk hand in hand. It hangs in stark contrast to the cultural milieu of a just-waking Bombay, ripe with different languages, tones, accents, sounds, scents, and lives. Pluralism in abundance, a cacophonic symphony.

Worlds Merging

"Come! I see Achie!!"

I spot my godmother across the lawn. I want to introduce Dustin to the woman who raised me and created a haven of love and safety for me in an otherwise tumultuous childhood. I want him to see where I inherited my love of singing my way through life, cooking meals with care, and being fiercely independent.

We are dressed for the wedding, and though Dustin's suit is entirely too warm in the Bombay sun, he's excited to meet family members he's only ever heard about.

My uncles, aunties, and cousins are all eager to know this *gora* I've brought home. Several queries are floated about when the two of us are planning to get hitched, with some cheekier relatives even getting ahead of themselves in the planning process:

"You can come here to get married. Don't worry about your Canadian friends. They'll see the photos. They get to see you all the time."

The sweetness of their love for me and my happiness is only slightly tinged with the bitterness that for me, home will always be between two worlds. It fills me with joy to know that Dustin straddles that divide with me, and as much as anyone can, understands more fully the bittersweetness of the in-between space I inhabit.

Achie stretches her arms out wide.

"*Aare*, my baby! Roselle! Baby! You're so thin. You're not eating?"

Immediately, Achie wants to feed me. This is her way. Food is love. A thin child is a sign of her not having loved hard enough. She whispers that she has biscuits in her bag if I want. She smells like coconut oil and Lux soap. Her embrace is home.

"Achie! Come. Come, I want you to meet Dustin."

I usher Dustin over. Achie is nervous. This is not territory she's ever waded into with me before. The last time I told her I liked a boy, I was much shorter than her, and she was making potato chops in the kitchen.

"*Tse tse*," she'd sucked on her tongue to show annoyance. "Don't let him sit on your head, huh? Boyfriend, foyfriend…you pay attention to your books!"

Distracted by my quest to steal a freshly-made potato chop, her response to my 11-year-old crush was moot.

"Achie. This is Dustin."

"*Nouro?*" she enquires in Konkani.

"*Voei*," I respond yes, even though it's not totally true; there's no parallel word for "partner" in Konkani so I affirm her calling him my husband.

"Hi, Achie." Dustin offers his hand.

Achie looks at him. She takes his hand with both of hers and leads him to a nearby parapet. I follow.

"*Voh boro ha!*" Still talking to me in Konkani, she signals her approval: he is good.

The two most important people in my life are meeting one another. The multiple truths of who I am exist in one sublime space. She, who has been with me from my very first day, and he who has promised to love me to my very last.

Still clutching his hands, Achie launches into a monologue that I am certain she has practiced before:

"She is my baby. I raised her. I took out her *kaka susu* Her mother is my sister, you know? She was hot-tempered, and she worked, and her Dada was always on the rigs. So I took care of baby, you know? I used to take her to school, feed her. She liked my potato chops and chow chow. Her mummy used to beat her lots, y'know. *Thak thak thak.*"

Achie's hands make a whipping motion through the air for emphasis.

"When her mother used to beat her, I used to take care of baby. She used to sleep in my bed, you know?"

My eyes well with tears at my truth being shared by someone else who was there. I hadn't misremembered my childhood. I had learned how to love from this incredible woman, this memory keeper.

Achie is shaken from her memories by the wedding usher, who guides us into the party hall. She gets us to agree to a visit before we leave Bombay in a few days.

The next few days fly by in a blur of family time, more food and whiskey than we can account for, and visits to ancient sites populated by errant street monkeys. On our last day in the city, Dustin and I head out to visit Achie in her home, where she said she wanted to cook for us.

The sweltering high noon hour creates a veritable maze of the gulleys of *Dhobi Talao*, especially since street signs and building numbers aren't standard fare. Lost, with no tech to help, we rely on the intrepid old-world ways of wayfinding: asking people. Thanks to a couple of street vendors, we finally find the right gully.

"Baby! Baby! Come come! Come up!"

Achie has spotted us from her perch on the second storey balcony, the entire top half of her body leaned over the railing, arms waving.

"I went to the bazaar first thing today and got big big pomfrets for you. I know they are your favourite, and I stuffed them with *rechaad masala*."

She stops, as if remembering something, and turns to Dustin.

"You like *rechaad masala*? It's not so *teekha*," she assures him the food isn't too spicy.

"I love *masala*!" Dustin chuckles.

"Come, come. Sit. I'll turn the fan on. You'll drink falooda, no?"

Achie serves us cold drinks that she's bought specially for us. I worry she's spent too much and gone to too much trouble.

"What trouble? You're my baby, and you've come home after so long. I only want to see you blessed."

Over lunch, a classic Goan meal of fish curry on parboiled rice, with Achie's stuffed fried pomfret, she tells us about her life and what's worrying her lately: her health, annoying neighbours, family drama. We eat with our hands because despite my programming that doing so is *ghatti* behaviour, that's how Achie's food tastes best. When we're finished, she insists we take seconds.

Our few hours with Achie zoom by. She insists that

we stay with her next time we're in town. I ask her if she wants to come with us to Canada.

"So far away, baby. My life is here. I am from here. You go, be good, huh? You come and see me next time. You stay here. I'll give you my bed."

There is no one like Achie in the world. Generous to a fault, and the most willing to love. As she walks us down to the street, she hugs us both. Dustin slips a small something into her hands. That is what we do in our culture. We present our elders with a token of our gratitude for the lifeblood they've poured into us. She looks at his gift, amazed.

"I'll pray for you both."

I know she will.

My worlds, which I have kept so carefully separated for so long, have merged. In their merging, perhaps I too can become whole.

No Justice, No Peace

"You're like a mad dog about this tile nonsense," my father spits at me.

I'm in the back seat of the van chatting with Dustin about finding a tile to replace the one my father threw away. My father's words, dripping with disdain, slice through me, and I fall silent. The silence is thick, and seems to satisfy his desire to stop hearing about this infernal tile.

Dustin and I left Bombay a few days ago and made our way to Goa. We're staying with my parents in their villa in the southern part of the state, close to the beaches that have made the place infamous the world over. I am least interested in the beaches on this trip. I crave a return to the place that I scoffed at visiting a decade ago: my ancestral home in the village of Ucassaim. I am hungry to replace the talisman of connection to my lost roots.

Since arriving in Goa, my father has made a healthy dent in a jerrican of homemade fenny, Goa's signature cashew-based moonshine. His afternoons and evenings are spent slurring and falling. At night he is comatose. Mornings are an exercise in punishment for those of us in the path of his cruelty-infused hangover, for which there is only one cure: lather, rinse, repeat.

I worried that my father's drinking schedule would squelch my plans of returning to Papa's house to find a tile. Now that we're almost there, I can hardly believe it.

Coming here now feels like a pilgrimage, a return to a sacred site. One that has become that much more meaningful since losing the piece of tile that I found a decade ago.

"I cannot take this poison with me to this sacred site," I think.

I inhale. A deep, lung-filling breath.

The air is sweet, warm. It is the same air that generations of my ancestors have breathed. My lungs full, feet grounded in my land, I turn back to where my father is sitting in the front seat of the van.

My ears ring in anticipation for what I'm about to do.

"Dad, you don't have to like it or agree with it, but the only reason I'm here is because you threw away the tile that I had. You don't have to understand why this is important to me, but you don't get to bully me about it."

"You're so sensitive," he says. "I was just joking. Don't take things so seriously."

I've stopped listening. For the first time in my own memory, albeit with a loud ringing in my ears and a tightness in my chest, I have said the exact thing I wanted to say in the exact moment in which I wanted to say it.

*

"I'm so tired of people like *her* coming to this country only to tear it down. If they don't like it here, just go somewhere else."

The man looked at me pointedly. I was the "her" he was referring to.

We had just exited a conference talk where I'd made a comment that he didn't agree with. At the national conference on diversity and inclusion–the landscape of my professional work– the panel talk showcased the lived experience of four racialized people. The panelists shared painful experiences of racism with a packed room of attendees, and had made reference to colonialism and the harms it continued to perpetuate on their lives and sense of belonging.

An audience member ambled to the microphone during the question period that followed the panel talk. "You might call it colonialism," he said, "but it was a gift, and you have to show some respect for the cultural tradition that those people brought here."

His words opened a pit and I felt myself falling. Despite the few hundred people in the room, I suddenly felt very alone. Blood rushed to my ears. My skin was hot. My heart raced. I could not shake off the sliminess of his comment.

In the room as a participant, a leader, and a panel speaker myself, I was compelled to say something, and I found myself standing shakily at the microphone:

"I will start by saying thank you for the intense amount of emotional, psychological and personal labour that goes into sitting up there and speaking your truth," I expressed to the courageous panelists. "A comment that was made compelled me to come to this microphone. I don't want to dissect the comment, but I do need to address that colonialism was not a gift. Colonialism was a destroyer of culture and heritage. It was a genocide and it continues to be so. [...] I believe the phrase, 'you should be grateful' was used. I'm sorry, but I am tired of being "should" all over. I *should* be grateful. I *should* be thankful for the gifts of colonialism. I am not."

The room erupted, and a majority of the attendees stood, clapping. My voice quivered, but it did not break.

In the minutes, hours, and months that followed, people from across the country would reach out to me. In person, via email, by text, and over social media channels. Most would tell me how proud they were of me, how they needed someone to say something, and that they were glad I did.

Others would contact me to let me know that I was the one who was sowing division. Like the man who expressed his tiredness at people like me coming to this country only to tear it down.

I said what I needed to say, and I'm proud that it resonated with some, and comfortable in the knowledge that my words had ruffled some feathers. It reminded me of the letter I had penned in my teens to the local newspaper when I had witnessed a similar injustice.

"Hey! Did I see you pulled over on Winston Churchill yesterday?" I had asked my friend and deskmate. "I thought I recognized your mom's car."

It was first period, and we were chatting in Calculus class, awaiting our teacher's lesson for the day.

"Yea. They just tailed me all the way from my house, and then just after those lights, they pulled me over. The first thing they asked me was, 'Where's the weed?'"

"What? That's ridiculous. You don't even speed!"

I had often teased my friend, who lived down the street from me and regularly drove us to school in his mother's car, for always adhering to the speed limit. I was livid at his experience, and wanted to take action. I thought to write a public letter about this injustice. Even then—long before the social (re)awakening for racial justice catalyzed by the murders of Trayvon Martin, Breonna Taylor, and George Floyd amongst so so many more—I knew in my bones that what my friend had experienced was because he was Black.

The Mississauga

Wednesday, June 18, 2003

Friend Stopped

Someone I know was pulled over for speeding on Winston Churchill Blvd., north of Burnhamthorpe recently.

However, it wasn't his speed that interested the undercover police officers who'd been following him since he'd left his home. Upon pulling my friend's relatively new car over, their first question to him was, "Where's the weed?"

Does the fact that my friend is Jamaican, a youngster and driving a nice car, automatically make him a dope-smoking criminal?

The fact that he's an honour roll, medical

school bound student shocked the police officers.

When the report on racial profiling came out in Toronto a few months ago I didn't believe it was accurate. I thought to myself, "We live in an educated society where people are judged by the goodness of their actions instead of the colour of their skins."

Boy was I ever naive!

The undercover cops not only stopped my friend under false pretences, but also searched his car for the drugs that any person fitting his description should

have on them.

I have always had faith in our institution of law-enforcement for their many wonderful officers. However, it is incidences like this that make me lose a little bit of faith in the true goodness of man.

Roselle Gonsalves
Mississauga

✱

My father's accusation that I am too sensitive is one that I've heard repeatedly throughout my life.

For so many years I believed this to be a terrible thing–something I needed to eradicate. I've come to understand, however, that my sensitivity is my strength. I am a person who cares. Deeply. About everything. I have always had opinions. Strong ones. I also have intense emotional reactions to the things about which I care deeply. Dustin teases me about my allergy to the term "easy-going."

Like many millennials, Dustin and I met online. My pet peeve on dating sites prior to meeting him had been people describing themselves as "easy-going," like some freaking badge of honour. It became so frustrating that if I saw it on their profile, they were automatically disqualified.

"Have a damn personality," I wanted to yell. "If I kidnap your dog, are you still going to be easy-going?"

Dustin did not describe himself as easy-going in his online profile, partly because he's not, and also because he expressed his personality in more than platitudinal clichés. He was compelling, earnest, opinionated. He still is.

When people describe themselves as easy-going, or chill, or low maintenance, or drama free, or whatever simplistic synonym applies, I wonder if what they're hoping to convey is that they're willing to make themselves as small as needed to be convenient enough to love. If we make ourselves small enough, then we don't have to fear that our partners and lovers and friends and loved ones will think of us as a burden. As too much. When people call us too sensitive or dismiss our voices as foolish, or tell us to go back to where we came from, what they are telling us is that our expression of self makes them uncomfortable.

I question if I am actually too much then, or whether that which aims to contain me is in fact too small?

The fear of being disliked is a deeply uncomfortable one. If one is disliked then it must mean that one is unlikeable. This fallacy is so deeply entrenched in our relationality that we've created an entire way of being in the world that demands that we contort ourselves into the tiniest pretzel version of ourselves, digestible morsels of personality, never inconveniencing the world around us. I want the people around me to impact me with their fullness, their authenticity, their big ideas and enormous passionate emotions. I believe we are big enough to hold space for each other's fullness.

I want to live in a world in which I too can take up space. I want to have an impact. I want my being to make ripples that roll out into the oceans and crash as waves on distant shores.

Heaven forbid my epitaph should ever read: "She was easy-going."

Keep Moving

The ringing in my ears is alarmingly loud as I turn away from the van that holds my parents. As I make my way through the untamed forest towards the house, I hear them:

"See? She's so disrespectful. What did I say? I was just joking. I can't say anything when she's in her moods. Always so sensitive."

"Leave me out of this. She's your daughter. I don't want to get in the middle."

My mother's response catches me. I realize that my willingness to stand against injustice is rooted in my umbrage at apathy in the face of said injustice. I have a deep-seated resistance to the myth of neutrality.

✳

As Dustin and I walked to the Lincoln Memorial one gloomy morning, the wind off the Potomac River whipped tears from my eyes. It was my first time in Washington DC, a place where the myth and promise of America are ever present. As we made our way through the many war memorials, our map told us that the Martin Luther King Jr. Memorial was closeby. I have a special fondness for MLK, ever since visiting his childhood home a dozen years ago in Atlanta. A parchment of his infamous *I Have a Dream* speech has sat with me in every workspace I have been in for over a decade now. His words, powerful and unrelenting, have guided me, offered me grace, strength, and wisdom when I have most needed them.

At the memorial site, a larger-than-life stone carving of Dr. King stood stoic, gazing over the Potomac towards the Jefferson Memorial on the other side. On the side of the rock, a quote:

"Out of the mountain of despair, a stone of hope."

Something within me moved, and I was unable to speak. It is the closest I have ever come to feeling on hallowed ground.

In my professional career I have often felt stymied by the sheer audacity of what can be done to bring about a better world. One in which systems of injustice are rectified. One in which our humanity is centered. These feelings of hopelessness loom large when the work seems too big, and the world too mired in its own oppression. Yet, standing in the presence of Dr. King, surrounded by his words on the walls that enveloped the memorial, I understood my life's calling: to set small stones on a path forged by the footsteps of giants.

I do not always feel strong or brave or resilient or capable. I am often scared, anxious, weak of voice, and trembling. I have often questioned the wisdom of shaping a career built on seeking justice, and have often considered abandoning it when the costs feel too high. Yet, as I stood at the memorial of a man whose actual life had been sacrificed to the service of humanity many years before my own birth, I was offered this wisdom, carved into a stone wall ahead of me:

> *Make a career of humanity. Commit*
> *yourself to the noble struggle for equal*
> *rights. You will make a greater person of*
> *yourself, a greater nation of your country,*
> *and a finer world to live in.*
> —*Dr. Martin Luther King Jr., District*
> *of Columbia, 1959*

This king had spoken these words in the place where I now stood. Somehow, I felt that he was speaking to me, encouraging me to lean into the discomfort of fighting for the rights of people who have been oppressed. After all, no one had said that living a purpose-driven life would be an easy row to hoe.

Dustin wrapped his arms around me, and I couldn't tell if my hot tears were from the frenzied wind whipping around me or the vortex of emotions roiling within.

After the memorial, we wound our way through the National Mall, past the White House, and to the Smithsonian's National Museum of African American History & Culture. The enormity of the building and sheer volume of the exhibits housed within, seemed daunting. The volunteer at the welcome desk suggested we start on the lower level, at the historical exhibitions, the first of which was entitled *Slavery and Freedom*.

In line to the entryway, I observed that the vast majority of people around me were African American. There was a very small handful of white folks, an even smaller number of people of East Asian heritage, and I seemed to be the only South Asian person in the whole museum. I could feel an angry energy rising up within me.

"Where are my people?"

Dustin was beside me, but my question was to the ether. Why were people who looked like me not here bearing witness to the history, lives, and oppressions of our Black siblings?

Knowing that anti-Blackness runs deep in non-Black racialized communities, and also that, as Dr. King said, none of us is free until all of us is free, I felt incensed at this glaring lack of presence.

As we descended into the exhibition on enslaved Africans, the air in the room took on a heaviness. It felt like everyone was holding their collective breath, knowing that where we stood held the stories of centuries and lives lost to oppression. In the cavernous space, we were surrounded by objects of significance. "Significance" seems too weightless a word to convey the sheer power and magnitude of that room. In one enclave, ballasts from the *São José*, a Portuguese ship that had brought enslaved Africans across the Atlantic Ocean. In another, the shackles found on the ship, both in adult and child sizes, for the slavers cared not what aged person they were enslaving.

I found myself in shock in the presence of these objects. Powerful talismans of the past that bore inconceivable trauma, pain, cruelty, and malignancy, whose tentacles continue to penetrate into our present day.

As I made my way past a showcase that held objects found aboard these ships, which housed an ornate blue and white bowl, I heard the white woman beside me exclaim:

"Oh wow. What a beautiful bowl. I hope they sell ones like it in the gift shop."

Unnerved at the callousness of such a comment in such a grave space, I found myself staring at a William Cowper quote etched on the glass in front of me: "I admit I am sickened at the purchase of slaves...but I must be mumm, for how could we do without sugar or rum?"

There have always been, and will always be, people who put their creature comforts—sugar, rum, a ceramic bowl from the gift shop—ahead of the humanity and dignity of the people around them.

I moved myself to another room to shake off the ugliness. A video was explaining the sheer volume of African peoples who were taken by European slavers away from their homes. The video played loudly on loop as we milled about the exhibit. It referred to the ships and their "precious cargo" on their journey across the Atlantic, and the millions of lives that were lost in the liminal waters between land masses.

A small Black child, no more than three or four years old, with pink beads in her hair, held her mother's hand. Enthralled by the giant waves on the screen, she turned to her mother and asked:

"Mama, what was on the ships?"

How can a mother explain to her child who and what was on those ships? How is she supposed to break her own heart and the veil of innocence that protects her baby?

Dr. King wrote in his letter from the Birmingham Jail: "Injustice anywhere is a threat to justice everywhere. We are caught in an inescapable network of mutuality, tied in a single garment of destiny. Whatever affects one directly, affects all indirectly."[1]

How can we look each other in the eye and continue operating as if nothing is wrong, when the through line of those ships continues to today, and the anti-Black world that that little girl will inevitably grow up experiencing is continually being perpetuated? How can we continue to put our efforts into building this world where my freedom is not completely wrapped up in the freedoms of the people around me?

I bristle at the idea that we can be passive observers to life passing us by. The idea of being neutral or apolitical is a deeply privileged one. Being removed from conversations that seem uncomfortable is only an ease that is offered to people who benefit from the extant power structures.

Many years from now, long after this trip to Goa with my parents and Dustin, on yet another phone call with my mother, one that hindisght would reveal to be our last, she will express her irritation at the ongoing calls for accountability and racial justice that will have become a big part of the cultural zeitgeist.

"I don't understand why these Blacks can't just do it like the rest of us. I'm coloured. I came to this country. You just have to work hard, and not be the victim."

"Mom! That is not true at all! And it's not a fair comparison at all. You migrated here by choice. You came to this country with money and had the privilege–" I don't get to finish.

"I think they're just different. Lazier, I think. Maybe not as smart."

"Mom, I don't think I can continue this conversation. I need to go."

1   King, Martin Luther, Jr. 2018. *Letter from Birmingham Jail.* Penguin Modern. London, England: Penguin Classics.

I will hang up, and vomit.

As Dustin and I made our way through the museum that day, I wept at the coffin of Emmitt Till, remembering the tiny Black girl with pink beads in her hair. Till was 14 years old when he was murdered in 1955. Nearly 60 years later, Michael Brown was 18 when he was murdered in 2014. In that same year, Tamir Rice was also murdered by police. He was 12 years old. How are Black children still being murdered? Where is our collective outrage?

My despair felt debilitating.

Then, as I ascended into the exhibit entitled *Making a Way Out of No Way*, like a stone of hope from a mountain of despair, Dr. King's voice boomed through the airscape:

We must keep moving. We must keep going.
If you can't fly, run.
If you can't run, walk.
If you can't walk, crawl.
But by all means…
Keep moving.

✱

I feel compelled to raise my voice against injustice in whatever ways are available to me: whether in a letter, at a microphone, or in a painful personal conversation. What a privilege it must be to choose to turn away from another's suffering, simply because it doesn't affect you.

It's why my mother's words about staying out of the clash between my father and I hurts me just as much as my father's cruelties. I cannot fathom what it must be like to remain apathetic.

Heading through the nettle-filled brush towards my ancestral home, I am overcome with a familiarly anxious energy for having spoken up for myself to my father. There is another feeling though–newer, more grounded–that I can only describe as awe. It feels like an answer to a question I didn't know was within me: that the injustices that I've witnessed and stood up to for so long, now finally also include my own experiences of harm.

My heart is pounding as I walk towards the ancient home. There is pain behind me, and something intriguing ahead of me. I hurry to create distance between the van and myself.

"Shake it off. You're here on a quest." Afraid that I've ruptured the balance of power, I encourage myself aloud to keep moving anyway.

The powerlessness my younger self often felt reappears now. What if I have upset my father too much? If I incur his wrath and retribution, I risk cutting this visit short.

Ahead of me, Dustin has whacked his way through the thorny overgrowth. In the clearing, the house comes into view. It is so starkly different than I recall, from just a decade ago.

To Dustin, it is a damn miracle that we are here at all. With pent up excitement finally released, he stretches out an arm, and beckons to me:

"C'mon! Let's go explore!"

Receiving Repair

There she is. The house. The last time I saw her, a decade ago, her walls were bright white. Now they are stripped down to the red brick. The teal wooden window shutters are gone, replaced by holes in the wall. The sun streaming through the space where the roof once was, seems incongruous to the decay.

Dustin peers into the holes that once were windows. I watch as he climbs through one, amazed at his gumption.

"There're snakes in there," I mindlessly echo the warning I'd been given as a small child. "Be careful!"

As the words leave my lips, I realize that I don't actually *know* that there are snakes in there. I simply believed what I was told decades ago, and that fear has kept me out all these years.

I believe firmly in the poetry of rupture and repair.

Like an egg that has to crack in order for a chicken to hatch. Like a bud that must burst for a flower to bloom. There are myriad examples in nature of this poetry. Almost as if life is set up to birth newness from the ashes of the old. If new ideas and ways of being are to emerge, I must also be willing to challenge old ideas that have remained unquestioned.

✳

Reconnecting after many years, Mel and I sat across from each other, awkward because it had been a few years since we'd seen each other. The catalyst for our separation had been an ill-fated fight, fueled by emotional weight, booze, and a panic attack (mine). Stubbornness (also mine) and self-righteousness (both of ours) allowed a once-thick friendship to stall, neither of us willing to bend first, rather preferring the break. It fed my own narrative at the time: "How could she? How dare she?"

Prior to that eruption, we'd been thick as thieves–graduate school friends, bonded in the muck of navigating the academic realm. She was one of the best minds I'd ever met: keen, delightful, hilarious, salty, sharp.

Her face looked different somehow now. Maybe the three years we'd been estranged had morphed my memory of a face that had once been so familiar. The diner was buzzing on that cold Wednesday night in January, a few weeks after a deeply contentious American election.

In the space between the election and inauguration, Mel had reached out with a simple text message to break the years-long stalemate: "Everything in the world feels too heavy right now. Wanna have dinner?"

Over dinner, we shared memories of drunken nights, and long philosophical talks. We were no longer those people though. We'd both gone through the fiery alley-ways of our respective graduate degrees, and come out on the other side, scorched. We'd both gotten jobs in the non-profit world, both lost and found people. How do you catch someone up on a life?

Like familiar strangers, over the next three hours we laughed, we mourned, we remembered, and we imagined a new and better way forward.

So many years have passed since all that. Today, Mel holds a place in my heart that is incomparable. She is a fierce champion, a trusted friend, an honest mirror. We tell it like it is to one another and simultaneously hold each others' hearts with tenderness and care. Vulnerability takes time for both of us, and having given ourselves that time, the gift of seeing and being seen is indescribable.

In some ways, the rupture that changed the trajec-tory of our relationship was a gift. If we hadn't had the opportunity to rebuild our relationship with intentional-ity, perhaps we would have continued being grad school friends, drifting off into differently shaped lives, keeping in touch once a year, hollowly promising to do so more often.

Instead, the intentional act of repairing what was once ruptured offered us the courage to co-create some-thing new, on the ruins of something old. Something that is now rooted in a foundation of trust, of truth, of accountability, of honesty, of love, of respect, of grace. This repair was a gift.

✳

Receiving the gift of relational repair has often been im-pacted by my own experiences of trauma and marginal-ization, because it is easier to close the portal to my open heart after a lifetime of having to shield myself from poison-tipped arrows.

Being able to receive what is good and positive, like gifts and praise, is entwined with my openness to receiving things that can feel scary, like critique or feedback.

For so many of us who've experienced life's hardships in inequitable ways, critical feedback can bring on a rush of self-flagellation and imposter syndrome. For instance, voluminous research exists on the experiences of racialized women, who are characterized in feedback conversations as intimidating, challenging, too intense, too direct, unsafe. These same traits expressed in less-melanated bodies are considered confident, business-savvy, and driven. All of the characterizations are rewarded and penalized accordingly.

In one such professional feedback conversation, my stomach clenched. It was my annual performance review, and I was nervous about what my boss was going to say.

She started speaking, touting my virtues, telling me what I was doing well.

"Come on already," I kept thinking. "Get to the point of all this. Where am I just absolutely dropping the ball?"

I knew all about the feedback sandwich: the good stuff was to butter me up before tearing me down. It was difficult for me to sit with her, reflecting on my positive attributes.

I waited for the real feedback. Finally, it arrived:

"There is something I need to bring to your attention," my boss began.

"Aha! I knew it!" I thought.

"I know you're really smart, but often I've noticed that you use words that nobody else knows and it kind of loses us when we can't understand you."

I felt sucker punched. There was no way for her to have known the deep wound that her words had re-opened.

I was too smart for my family of origin, and was reminded repeatedly of this.

"Remember, I gave you your brain, so you don't get to use it on me."

"You can keep all your degrees in a dustbin before you come into my house."

I was simultaneously penalized and mocked for being too smart but not cunning enough.

"Your intelligence means nothing."

I heard my boss's words through the echo of these deep wounds. Like the thousandth papercut on an unhealed swamp of the nine hundred and ninety nine papercuts beneath it.

I went home and stewed.

"How dare she tell me I'm too smart?"

She was demonizing me for a part of myself that I not only had no control over, but which had also been weaponized against me for so long. It was as though she was in cahoots with all the tormentors of my past. An army of antagonists, whose singular goal was to bring me pain.

My martyr syndrome came out in full force: "Fine! I'll just use two syllable words and make myself as digestible as possible."

It isn't within my nature to make myself smaller or more digestible though. If it was, I would have figured out a way to do so by now.

I had to reckon with the feedback. If what my boss was saying was true, then how I spoke was acting as a barrier to what I wanted to communicate.

At our next meeting, I asked my boss if she would watch for a behaviour modification I wanted to implement. "I've been thinking a lot about what you said about my use of language that might make it tough for others to follow." I did not let her into the serpentine mental process I'd been through since our last meeting.

"I am going to practice doing something: I'd like to say something as it comes naturally to me, and then I'd like to follow it with, '...and what I mean by that is...' so that I can offer a more accessible translation. Would you watch for me doing that and tell me if it lands?"

Framing my language translation as an exercise in accessibility allowed me to recognize that if my goal was to achieve audience buy-in, then equitable language would have to be a part of how I communicated. It didn't mean that my vocabulary would shrink, or that I would be less than myself, simply that I was committing to creating more expansive ways of being in and with the world around me.

In the thick of my self-righteous triggered ire however, I felt like I'd been asked to annex a core part of myself.

"Leave your brain at the door if you want to be a part of this family."

Not only was this untrue, but I have come to understand that if I don't take the time to heal my wounds, I will bleed all over people who haven't cut me.

This lack of ability to receive has often meant that it takes me exponentially longer to trust those around me: my friends, my partner, my colleagues, and perhaps most tragically, myself.

Having leaned into the truth of my trusted reflections over time, I've learned that my mechanisms of self-protection and preservation act as ways of keeping me safe. Safe from the danger of having to experience or re-experience harm. Rupture hurts! I have come to honour the protection of these ways, maladaptive though they may be. What I now also know to be true, is that letting people in, showing them my vulnerability, my heart, my authenticity, my sensitivity, has allowed me the great good fortune of being my most free and authentic self. The walls built to keep myself safe from the fear of rupture and pain may serve to keep harm out, but if unattended, they also inadvertently end up blocking out the ability to receive.

To receive kindness, generosity, truth, goodness, love.

To receive repair.

I am Good

Dustin ignores my baseless fear about snakes. I watch in awe, as he hops into Papa's house. Fuelled by his tenacity, I also launch myself through the window.

Thick cobwebs tickle my face as I pick my way through the vines and rubble of this crumbling estate. I imagine what it might have been like for my great-grandmother to receive visitors on her *balcão*. The pillars that stood stoic when I last visited, ten years ago, now lie in heaps of broken stones. I see no roof tiles anywhere. This has been a futile quest. Other than the bare brick walls, very little remains.

I trip and grab onto a thorny vine to steady myself. Sharp needles pierce my palms. This place is equal parts myth and mayhem.

Each flank of the house has a long corridor that

connects the front areas to the back. I look for clues in the piles of dirt and bramble. Maybe I'll find furniture or clothing– something that's escaped the ravages of time.

Did Papa's parents die here? I feel overwhelmed by all the stories lost, everything I will never know. Who were these people from whom I stem, but to whom I have nothing more than mere wisps of connection? Is there anything about me that reflects who they were?

Feeling the weight of my unanswerable questions, I make my way to the central chamber of the house. Even overrun by flora, there is no question that I am standing in my great-grandmother's kitchen, the hearth of this once grand home. I clear the bushes to reveal the *chulla*, a wood burning stove. I imagine putting wood into the cavern beneath. Breathing deeply, I lay my hands on the stove, picturing with sparkling clarity my great-grandmother baking her bread loaves here. Grinding her *masalas* on the *fator*.

✳

Food is the language of love that I inherited from Achie. Shopping, planning, prepping, cooking, and eating are all loving processes that have given me peace and joy. Until Dustin noticed my exuberance in my kitchen, the first time he visited my little apartment, it had never occurred to me that the love that Achie had infused into her food, continued to feed me in ways unknown.

My kitchen offers my heart the space to reflect on that which attempts to break it. These days, I reflect a lot on the ugliness of the world around us, like the protectionism that has reared its villainous head the world over. Protectionism, rooted in fear, is an illusion that values me over a separate you, us over a demonized them, here over an imagined there.

You cannot have what is mine.
Closed minds, closed borders, closed hearts.

One afternoon, as I spent the better part of an hour lovingly caramelizing the shallots that formed the base of a pasta dinner, I thought about how micro acts of love–cooking, eating, feeding another, sharing recipes–were the roots of a movement. A movement to combat, in the most human way, the scaredy-cat *rakshasa*, demon, of protectionism. In caramelizing the onions, I was following Achie's mandate to not skimp out on the *bagaar*.

As I tended to the *bagaar*, nice and long, just like Achie'd taught me, it dawned on me that my mother was a scared person. I scared her. Even in my child form, I was bigger and bolder and more assured of myself than she'd been allowed to be. The circumstances of her own intersectional identity had molded her with fear, shaped her to attack that which threatened to take away what she'd fought for–protectionism, even if towards her own child.

In my kitchen, I have come to know that the only medicine for fear is love. My recipes more often than not have instructions that sound more like old-world directions: a little bit of this, a splash of that, maybe some of that, but only if you have it.

These directions are based on generations of us knowing that it has always been less about the what and how of cooking that makes it meaningful. Instead, it has always been about the why. The why was, and always will be, love.

Over the last few years, my love of food has found me digging deeper into the lost pages of my matrilineage. I have often struggled to hear the voices of my ancestors. I don't know their names or faces or voices or stories. Colonized histories don't afford such remnants.

There is family lore that I remember fadingly now. Of my great-grandmother, a woman of great repute in Ucassaim, where the family operated the local bakery. She was strict, I'd heard. *Khadoos*, ruthless, may have been the word. Hardworking. Not very maternal, but loved her children in her own way: her seven daughters and her precious eighth, a boy child, whom I only ever knew as my Papa.

There are no pictures of Kosumai, that's what they called her. I guess I don't even have a name. Nameless and faceless, nevertheless, I feel her with me in my kitchen. I think of her as my hands knead and roll and stir and feed.

Once, during the semester in which I was teaching a university course on fat phobia and intersectional feminism, I knew that the week's discussions were about to take us through some particularly thorny territory around poverty and food trauma. I baked bread for my students. I recalled how special I'd felt at six years old when Teacher Francesca fed me at her birthday lunch. In preparation for my own class, my hands were lured by the siren song of flour and dough and warmth.

Kosumai was with me as I created this nourishment. I had been untethered from her by all manner of tangible record. Yet, somewhere deep in my bones was a river of memory that I did not recall. It seems it has been there always, waiting for me to listen.

From Kosumai through Achie to me and to the students in my classroom. As we chewed on those freshly baked loaves, slathered in homemade jam, we talked about sustenance and justice and peace.

After that class, I went to a therapy session, where I sat surrounded by the blankets and bolsters and props that were used to create physical safety for me as I processed my emotions. My therapist and I had been working for nearly a year on my core fear: that although I didn't think I was a bad person, I feared a more sinister version of myself–the one only my parents saw–lurked beneath the surface.

In a previous session, I'd articulated this fear: "Maybe my badness is so manipulative that I've tricked everyone around me, even myself, into believing I'm not a bad person. Maybe someday, without my knowledge and against my will, I'll become truly evil."

That day after class, I told my therapist about the bread I took to feed my students. I told her about how I had taken Achie and Teacher Francesca and Kosumai with me. I shared how my students had eaten and wept as we talked about difficult things from a place of nourishment. I told her that I felt accomplished and not at all like an imposter. Not like a bad child pretending to be good.

"What do you think that means?" she asked me tenderly.

My body heaved, tears streaming. Something seemed to shift.

"I don't know. I mean, maybe I'm good at what I do?"

"Yes, you are certainly very good at what you do. Is there something deeper that you think this might mean?"

I looked at her, not daring to believe what I was about to say. I exhaled the weight of all that had aimed to drown my voice.

"I guess. Maybe. I *am* good."

Touching Kosumai's *chula* now feels like I'm at a pilgrimage site. The bright sunshine filters its way through the vines and finds my face. I have never felt this degree of wholeness: under my feet, the place where my people have been for centuries, a few feet away from me, a partner who has seen all my wounds and has supported me with love as I seek healing and wholeness.

Filled with a sweet gratitude, I notice a half-walled cubicle beside the stove. I can hear the "aashaa gushaa aaaaa" of my Papa bathing me in my earliest memory. I imagine the pots of hot water boiled on the stove, for bath time. I am suspended between the here and now of my own time, and my imaginings of what this space was like when it had life coursing through it.

I imagine my Papa, himself once a little boy–the most precious and wanted child of this high-caste family, doted on by his parents and his seven elder sisters. I wonder if the rebellion that led him to leave this grandeur behind as a teenager was a part of him even as a child. Did his elders giggle nonsense syllables at him as they doused him in a delicious stream of perfectly warm water, heated on the *chula* in front of which I now stand? I am chuffed to consider the poetry of my oldest and most precious memory also perhaps being one of his: like bookends holding together two long and entwined storybooks.

As I step away from the stove, a vine whips out from under me, and I yelp. It is entirely too snakelike for my comfort. In all my exploration through the ruins of the home though, I have yet to see signs of any animal life, nevermind an actual living snake.

I leave the kitchen area and come upon an enormous well peering up at me, empty now where once I imagine it was filled with fresh delicious water. A family well beckons to family wealth. Less affluent families would have shared in the village well. I feel the weight of familial sorrow at the now-dry well, and the yester-fortunes it tells of.

Lost in the deep recesses of my mind, invented memories spiriting me down a river that my ancestors forged, I am startled when Dustin comes up behind me. I had lost him when we were exploring the back part of the house. His reappearance feels surreal: a human figure piercing an impenetrable fog in a Dickensian scene.

"Look! It's the kitchen. That there is the *chula*. And that's where you'd put wood to burn for it. Isn't that so cool? And look look. Here's the well. I can't believe we're standing here!" My exuberance overflows.

"That's incredible! I can't believe it either. What a cool place this is. Did you get a photo of the kitchen? We should put a picture of it in our kitchen at home."

I have been so focussed on replacing the lost tile, that I haven't considered alternative ways of bringing a part of this home back with me. I love the idea, and start taking photographs. Dustin waits while I finish.

"By the way," he says. "I think I found something for you."

I turn towards him as he pulls something out from behind his back.

Baked red clay, formed over a century ago. Stamped with the tilemaker's signature: *I Fernandes, Tileworks*.

A fully intact roof tile.

Unhurt. Unstruck. Unbroken.

Home

The rest of our time in India flies by.

The day before Dustin and I return to Canada, is our fifth anniversary. Half a decade of building a beautiful life of safety and love. We celebrate by hanging out on the beach all day, eating fresh seafood, drinking Kingfisher beers, and smoking cigars. When the sun begins its descent over the salty sea, we make our way to a tiny roadside shack for dinner.

It isn't fancy. The soft glow of candles is born of necessity because the electricity has gone kaput, and isn't expected to return for a few hours. It is perfect. The food is scrumptious.

On our way back to my parent's villa, we pass a bakery.

"Oooh. Let's stop and get some cake!"

My love of Black Forest Cake and Dustin's sweet tooth make this a compelling proposition. As I savour my slice, I take in the incredible human sitting across from me, and the good fortune of having him see all the parts of me that I spent my younger years worrying would be too "other."

I head back to the cake display.

"Can I have two slices to go, please? One Black Forest and one Raspberry Vanilla."

"We're getting more cake?"

"No no. This is for my parents. My dad loves Black Forest, and my mom loves vanilla."

We meander through the warm night air, back to the villa, with our baked treats. The lights are on. My mother, tucked away in her bedroom, glares at us through the open door when we enter the house.

The air is thick with tension, and my chest tightens as a vestigial part of my brain prepares itself for what is coming. My auto response is to wonder what I've done wrong.

"Hey dad, how you doing?" I am on high alert.

My father is pouring another glassful of fenny for himself in the kitchen. He slurs and sways like a long-limbed coconut tree hanging precariously in the wind.

"How was your anniversary dinner, guys?"

"Good, dad. We brought you a slice of Black Forest cake."

My father's big brown eyes, the ones I have so proudly inherited, are glassy and bloodshot, unable to focus on me. I guide him to the kitchen table, and ask if he wants to eat something.

"Cake. I'll have cake."

"Mom, I got you something sweet too," I call out to

her. "Want to come eat with us?"

I have slipped seamlessly into my preordained role of trying to make everyone happy. There is no response from my mother.

My father shovels the cake into his mouth with his hand, ignoring the spoon I try to give him. The word *ghatti* floats its way through my mind. There is no joy to be had in the cake.

Dustin and I go up to our room and pack. My heart hurts at the tableau I've left behind. I know now that I can never fix it. It was never mine to fix in the first place.

✳

A van arrives to take Dustin and me to the airport. In the driveway, I thank my parents for inviting us to India.

"Mom, I left your cake in the fridge, ok? Dad already ate his."

"I had cake?" My father doesn't remember the night before.

I kiss my mother goodbye, and wrap my arms around my father. My head still only reaches the middle of his chest. He will always be a giant of a man to me. In my imagination, I will hold tight to the memory of a cowboy-loving roughneck who smells of aftershave and Marlboros. Voice cracking, and hoping the dammed tears don't spill, I breathe him in one last time:

"Be good, dad."

I hold Dustin's hand all the way to the airport, very few words between us. I no longer fear that he will think less of me because of the behaviour of my parents. My heart still hurts for the rupture of my relationship with them, but it is no longer my shame to bear.

At the Bombay airport, we enjoy our last cup of *ka-*

dak chai. This feels so different to my panicked wait in the Delhi airport a decade ago.

"Oooh. Let's go to that gift shop. I think I see something that your ma will like," I tell Dustin.

I am excited to return to Canada and tell our family and friends of our trip. I feel proud of this place in which I am rooted, from where I come. I know now that India will always be here, as she has been for millenia. Perhaps more importantly, I now know that she will always be within *me.*

✳

"We flew through Heathrow when we first moved to Canada too. It was such a different airport then. I think I slept on some plastic yellow chairs because our layover was like eight hours long or something."

My immigration story is not new to Dustin. He's heard it so many times over the years. For those of us from oral traditions, retelling stories over and over is how we make meaning of them. It's how they live on for generations. I'm proud to partake of this ancient tradition.

At the airport, awaiting our next flight, I leave Dustin with our bags in a comfy seating pod to get myself a caffeine fix.

Standing in line at the cafe, I am enthralled by the absolute cacophony of humanity that swirls around me. Languages from all over the globe. Faces and shapes of lives I'll never touch. I'm feeling decidedly sentimental.

"Hi. What can I get for you?"

It's my turn to order.

"A grande americano with soy milk please."

"Do you want the milk heated?"

"No, thank you!"

I tap my phone on the payment kiosk, and wait.

"Where are you from?" the barista asks me.

An airport is guaranteed to be the one place where almost everyone is from somewhere else, so I don't mind.

"I'm Canadian but I was born and raised in India."

"Aap hindi bolte hain?"

(Do you speak Hindi?)

I am taken aback at her question.

"Haan! Tum bhee? Mujhe laga ki aap Cheen se hain!"

(Yes! You too? I thought you were maybe Chinese!)

I had coded the woman across the counter as being of East Asian origin.

"Nahin, nahin. Main Nepali hoon, lekin main bachpan se Khalapur mein rehta tha. Aur, main cheh maheene se yahaan hoon. Aap kaha se hai?"

(No, no. I'm Nepali, but I have lived in Khalapur since childhood. I've been here for six months. Where are you from?)

"Mein Bumbai se hoon, lekin mein bachpan me Canada gayaa tha. Khalapur...voh Lonavala ke paas hai na?"

(I'm from Bombay, but I went to Canada in childhood. Khalapur...that's near Lonavala no?)

"Aapko Lonavala maaloom hain?"

(You know Lonavala?)

"Haan! Bachpan mein hum wahan jaate the...holiday ke liye!"

(Yes! In childhood, we used to go there...for holidays!)

"Vah! Bumbai mein, aap kahan rehte the? Mera maa-baap ka dukaan VT Station ke paas tha."

(Wow! Where in Bombay were you from? My parents had a store near VT Station.)

"Mein Baandra se hoon."

(I'm from Bandra.)

The other barista is starting to throw some salty looks our way. We've dived into the deep with our conversation–two familiars in a foreign land.

"*Chalo, mein jaungi. Aapka naam kya hain?*"

(Come on, I'll leave. What is your name?)

"Sonam."

"*Sonam! Mein* Roselle *hoon.*"

(Sonam! I'm Roselle)

"*Aapse milkar bahut achchha laga, Roselle. Aap meri behain ke jaisi ho.*"

(It was so good to meet you, Roselle. You are like my sister.)

To have found recognition and connection in this liminal space feels surreal.

I grab my drink and wave goodbye to Sonam, floating all the way back to Dustin.

"You're not going to believe this…"

✸

The flight from Heathrow to Toronto's Pearson International is an echo of the one I flew almost exactly 20 years ago. Thirteen years old, and smitten with Matt Damon, I watched *Good Will Hunting* on that flight. The suitcase packed with all my favourite books and mementos from my life in India was permanently lost in the vacuum between the old country and the new one. Remembering that now, I am overcome by fear: what if my checked luggage on *this* flight is lost? The ultra-precious roof tile that Dustin found for me just last week is in my suitcase. Attempting to quell my worry, I am reminded that my 13-year-old self survived the loss of her precious things two decades ago. In remembering her resilience, I too am calmed at the fear of losing the tile on this journey.

What would I tell my younger self?

I would thank her for bringing her spirit of adventure and love of people with her, because now I get to have pieces of those gifts with me too. I would warn her of the impending loss of all her precious things, and let her know that it is alright for her to grieve those losses.

I would tell the girl who made this journey those many years ago that she's not a bad girl. That she doesn't need to reinvent herself in order to be loved or lovable. I want her to know that she can trust her own voice. Her willingness to see and speak the truth is something that I remain so very grateful for.

I'd want her to know that she ends up having a really freaking awesome life, with her own home and a dog and yes, even a boy who loves her to the moon. That in her future home, there is no screaming, no hitting, no drunken fights. I'd want her to know that she will find peace.

I want to thank her for her courage, her hilarity, her intelligence, her curiosity, her love of quirky people, her scrappiness, and her willingness to stand up for what's right.

As I stare out the window, suspended in the space between me and her, I whisper across the planes of time: "Thank you for being you, so that I could be me."

I pull myself out of my reverie and put on *The Sound of Music*, a perennial favourite. I know all the words by heart and lip sync to Fraulein Maria wondering what good she must have done in her wicked childhood to have found such love in her life.

Dustin notices me faux-singing and squeezes my hand. The fears I've had of being unlovable seem to have had their edges smoothed over time by the consistent current of allowing love in. Being seen is a tremendous thing.

I have stopped waiting for the other shoe to drop.

＊

Being seen fully by those around me has afforded me the good fortune of seeing myself more clearly. Of being more honest about my warts, and about my gifts. Of being un-apologetic for my brightness, and being cognizant of my crunchier bits. I have recovered parts of myself long for-gotten at the bottom of the ocean.

It's easy to imagine that I was saved: by Dustin, by my beautiful friends. I think it's a bit deeper than that. I think letting other people in to see me in my wholeness has created reflections of myself that have allowed me to know myself more fully. To integrate those pieces of my-self into a more complete picture.

Over time, I have come to know that it is in the space between the two beats of a heart where I find meaning, giving heft to what comes before and after, and connecting one to the other. In these interstitial spaces, I search for what my heart yearns for: connection, relation, belonging. I am more authentically me because I've chosen to let other people see me and love me, and that has permeated every area of my life.

As my life has grown and taken me into spaces and in directions that allow me to lean into my bigness, my brightness, my boldness, I remain tethered to that which keeps me whole: those spaces of trusted relationships where I can take off the stage make-up and put on my sweatpants. Behind every accomplishment is the value of authenticity in my dearest relationships, the ones that offer me true reflections of myself.

In a world that, for me, has been shaped by the un-derstanding that in order for me to be loved and loveable, I needed to fit into someone else's idea of who and what

I should be, allowing myself to be seen fully by another is a scary thing. It is courageous to reveal myself, and it is revolutionary to have someone bear witness to my fullness, and not turn away.

I grab Dustin's hand when we arrive in Toronto, and together we head over to clear customs.

"Where are you coming from?" asks the border agent.

"India."

"How long were you gone?"

"Two weeks. We were there for a family wedding and some sightseeing."

The agent stamps our passports and hands them back to me with a small smile.

"Welcome home."

ACKNOWLEDGEMENTS

*"If each of my words were a drop of
water, you would see through them
and glimpse what I feel: gratitude,
acknowledgement."*

—Octavio Paz
Nobel Lecture 1990

The writing of this book saw me shed more tears, feel more grief, and taste more joy than I ever thought possible. I am grateful to each person who has afforded me the space and grace to experience all of this, and more.

Thank you to the incredible developmental manuscript readers, for your generosity and feedback, which helped bring this dream to life: Abby Bajuniemi, Ariel Eve, Hannah DiNardo, Larry Yoder, MaryAnn Ofodum, Megan Bartel, and Nekolina Lau.

A note of special thanks to Elaine Crume, whom I was so honoured to have as an early reader of this book because of the front-row seat we've had to each others' stories for 20+ years. From the day we met on the world wide web, I have felt recognized in you, my cosmic doppelganger.

Thank you to the effervescent Lindy Pfeil: writing coach, confidante, editor extraordinaire, twin soul. Our weekly early-morning check-ins were a cornerstone of this writing process for me. Even when I doubted it, you believed in putting these words into the world. Your gentle and purposeful guidance cultivated the safety I needed to set my truths free.

Many of the stories in the book had only ever been

shared in the sanctity of a counseling session. Thank you to Dr. Judy Chew, Anna Harland, and Melissa Schmode-Kristoff, each exemplars of the healing profession, for your invaluable work, which has afforded me the ability to trust my own body, and listen to my own voice.

I am fortunate for the blessings of good relations: Teresa-Anne Martin, Jessica Orcutt. Heather Gallant, Brandon Gallant, and Christie Mellan. Thank you for your love, through the storms and the sunshine. You've given me the freedom to be my fullest self–to fly and to fall, knowing that I can always come home to you.

To my Papa and Achie, neither of whom will ever read this book: this is the continuation of your story and legacy. Thank you for showing me how to love. I carry you both in my heart, as my guide and protector.

I felt a part of me break when Zeke Gonsalves-Smith crossed the rainbow bridge in 2022. I am forever grateful for the heart-expanding love that he has left me with. It was the honour of my life to be his human.

Finally, to my kind-hearted, courageous, brilliant partner Dustin Smith. Words seem a shallow vessel to hold the depth of my gratitude for you. If someone had asked me as a child to imagine the most incredible version of my future, that vision wouldn't hold a candle to the life you and I have built together. Thank you for holding all of my heart with such tenderness—and for trusting me with yours in return. It is the honour of my life to be your person. Beyond words, languages, and lifetimes, I love you.

Manufactured by Amazon.ca
Bolton, ON

36243074R00149